ISBN 978-1-332-03732-2
PIBN 10273779

This book is a reproduction of an important historical work. Forgotten Books uses
state-of-the-art technology to digitally reconstruct the work, preserving the original format
whilst repairing imperfections present in the aged copy. In rare cases, an imperfection in
the original, such as a blemish or missing page, may be replicated in our edition. We do,
however, repair the vast majority of imperfections successfully; any imperfections that
remain are intentionally left to preserve the state of such historical works.

For support please visit www.forgottenbooks.com

1 MONTH OF
FREE
READING

at
www.ForgottenBooks.com

By purchasing this book you are eligible for one month membership to ForgottenBooks.com, giving you unlimited access to our entire collection of over 1,000,000 titles via our web site and mobile apps.

To claim your free month visit:

www.forgottenbooks.com/free273779

English
Français
Deutsche
Italiano
Español
Português

www.forgottenbooks.com

Mythology Photography **Fiction**
Fishing Christianity **Art** Cooking
Essays Buddhism Freemasonry
Medicine **Biology** Music **Ancient
Egypt** Evolution Carpentry Physics
Dance Geology **Mathematics** Fitness
Shakespeare **Folklore** Yoga Marketing
Confidence Immortality Biographies
Poetry **Psychology** Witchcraft
Electronics Chemistry History **Law**
Accounting **Philosophy** Anthropology
Alchemy Drama Quantum Mechanics
Atheism Sexual Health **Ancient History**
Entrepreneurship Languages Sport
Paleontology Needlework Islam
Metaphysics Investment Archaeology
Parenting Statistics Criminology
Motivational

The Two Orations on the Crown.

ÆSCHINES

AND

DEMOSTHENES.

A NEW TRANSLATION.

BY

GEORGE W. BIDDLE.

PHILADELPHIA:
J. B. LIPPINCOTT & CO.
1881.

ADVERTISEMENT.

ANOTHER translation of the Orations on the Crown is here presented. Many English translations already exist, but an attempt is now made to unite sufficient literal adherence to the original with what may be called the forensic tone of the occasion.

This version is not incumbered with notes, nor prefaced with an elaborate introduction. Attention is simply called to the political condition of Greece, and to the principal circumstances of the trial, and a slight comparison of the two orations is made. The reader who desires more will find all needed information in the introduction to Kennedy's translation of the Oration of Demosthenes, and in the editions of the Greek text of that oration of T. K. Arnold and Arthur Holmes.

♪⌒)

INTRODUCTION.

FROM the time that Demosthenes first entered public life he regarded Philip with distrust. He recognized his wonderful abilities, and foresaw that unless his policy was counteracted, the Grecian States would one by one be swallowed up by him, and that instead of free, autonomous, independent States, they would all become members of a great empire under the Macedonian hegemony. Athens, which from the battle of Salamis had been the leader of Greece, and which though now shorn of much of her ancient power and authority was still foremost among the leading States, w uld be compelled to descend from her pre-eminence as guardian of the Hellenic liberties, and subside into a subordinate position. His patriotism shrank from such a view, and he may be said to have been for many years the leader of the anti-Macedonian party, ever on the alert to watch, proclaim, and oppose the designs of Philip, and to stir up the

Athenians to take active measures against him. Probably a majority of the Athenians were on his side; but the people were unwilling to undergo the labors and to submit to the sacrifices which the duty of opposing Philip's ambitious views demanded. They were moreover sustained in their feelings of apathy by a considerable number of respectable leaders. Among these the most prominent were the virtuous Phocion, and Æschines. The former honestly believed his fellow-citizens were incapable of resisting the Macedonian power; the latter had perhaps become a member of the pro-Macedonian party from interested motives. The battle of Chæronea, which took place in August of the year 338 B.C., and which was probably precipitated by Demosthenes, put an end forever to all hopes of successfully resisting Philip.

After this fatal battle Athens took hastily some measures of defence, which the peace, concluded a few days later, made unnecessary. One of these measures, however, was not abandoned, namely, the repair of the walls of Athens and of Piræus, a considerable work, which involved an expenditure of one hundred talents, or about $120,000 of our money.

This was resolved upon early in the year 337,

upon the motion of Demosthenes, and a commission of ten citizens, one drawn from each tribe, was appointed in the summer of the same year to carry the resolution into effect. Demosthenes, representing the tribe Pandion, was on this commission, and took charge of a section of the work forming about a tenth of the whole.

He added out of his own funds the sum of three talents to the amount drawn from the public treasury for this service, and moreover contributed liberally from his private resources to the Theoric Fund for the maintenance of public spectacles, of which he was administrator.

The work was completed and the commission executed in the year following, 336. Ctesiphon, a member of the Council of Five Hundred, and a friend of Demosthenes, then introduced a decree that a crown of gold should be publicly bestowed upon him in the theatre, at the celebration of the great Dionysiac festivals, the usual reward of public services and functions honorably performed. It was in the form of similar decrees, and provided that proclamation should be made by the herald that Demosthenes was crowned by the Athenian people for the virtue and good-will always shewn by him both in speech and action in his country's behalf. Brief and simple as this formula was, it appeared to imply, under the circumstances, an approval of Demosthenes's whole political course, and to be a protest against the Macedonian hegemony.

When, therefore, this decree, after its passage by the Five Hundred, was presented to the Assembly for concurrence, it was opposed by Æschines on the ground of illegality both in form and substance, and a prosecution was in consequence instituted against Ctesiphon, styled the *Graphe Paranomon.* The formal objections were that no such decree could be passed while the accounts of a public officer remained unsettled, and as Demosthenes had not yet had his accounts audited as a member of the Wall Commission and as Administrator of the Theoric Fund, the proposed coronation was illegal. Furthermore, the coronation as proposed could not be made in the theatre at all, but must be done at the Pnyx during the holding of an Assembly. The objection of substance struck at the orator's whole political life. It was contended that as nothing untrue could be introduced into a public record, and as it was false that Demosthenes had always by speech and action done what was best for the interests of the people, the decree was illegal and void, and its propounder guilty.

This occurred in the year 336, a few days before Philip's death, but the trial remained suspended for more than six years, and was not taken up until the year 330. The cause of the delay has not been explained. Perhaps the prosecutor waited for the most favorable. time to bring the trial on, and Ctesiphon and his friends might naturally not be averse to delay.]

Be the reason what it might, nothing was done until after the battles of Issus and Arbela, when Alexander, having conquered the Persians, was preparing to advance to the Indus. The moment was judged favorable, and the cause began before a jury of five hundred dicasts, or jurors.

' Æschines, on behalf of the prosecution, spoke first, pronouncing the discourse which still survives. He presented the legal points with great force and ability, and then launched into a violent personal and political attack upon his rival. The whole public career of Demosthenes was harshly examined, and it was endeavored to be shewn that his policy had from the first been unfortunate for the interests of Athens, until it culminated in the fatal battle of Chæronea. On the other hand the

moderation of both Philip and Alexander was
praised; and the speaker claimed merit for his
intimacy and friendship with them.

The most bitter personal assault was also made
upon Demosthenes, his parentage and his private
life and habits being grossly slandered, and cowardice attributed to him on the day on which
Athens had need of the valor of all her sons.
Æschines even reproached his adversary with his
ill-fortune, and asserted that nothing ever contrived by him had succeeded, since the Gods themselves were against him.

Ctesiphon defended himself in a few words, and
then Demosthenes arose and pronounced what by
universal acclaim is regarded as the most perfect
of orations.

He began by demanding of his judges the right
to arrange and present his arguments in the order
which he deemed most convenient, and after a
solemn invocation to his country's Gods to inspire
his hearers to listen to him with the same benevo-
lence they had ever shewn him, he gave a rapid
but masterly sketch of the condition of Athens at
the time peace was concluded in the year 347,
proving that the venality of Æschines and his fellows had helped Philip in his attempt to get the

control of Greece. He next touched briefly but emphatically the technical points of the cause; and after replying with great severity to the personal assaults made upon him, contrasting the private life and fortune of Æschines with his own, he finally passed in review before the jury his whole political life. His policy it is true had not succeeded, Athens had succumbed and the Macedonian was triumphant. But had the City committed a mistake in striving to repress Philip's ambitious efforts, and to preserve her leadership in Greece? As he warmed up he even asserted that had the result been foreknown to all, Athens must still have acted as she had, having due regard for herself, her ancestors, and posterity. The issue had been decided against her, but her glories though dimmed were still preserved.

The trial was one of the greatest ever known. It was in reality the conflict between the advocates of independence on the one hand and the upholders of submission on the other. All Greece was present and pressed round the platform from which the orators declaimed. The result was creditable to the sense of justice of the Athenians, and shed a dying ray of light upon the City which dared, in spite of the insolence of power, to give a verdict in accordance with truth and honor. Ctesiphon was acquitted by an immense majority, Æschines not obtaining a fifth part of the votes, which was necessary to protect him from fine. He went into voluntary exile, and it is said his rival aided him from his own purse when he left the City.

Impartial criticism will, it is thought, regard Demosthenes as single-minded, pure, and patriotic in the course which he advocated. And it may be asserted that this course was by no means the unwise one which Phocion believed it to be, and which Æschines asserted it was. Had the Athenians had a general such as Epaminondas, or had Phocion himself commanded at Chæronea, the result would probably have been different, the power of Philip might have been broken, and the decline of Athens for a long time stayed. We need not however speculate further as to this. What we are concerned with here is the political character of the great orator, and the manner of his defence of himself. Mr. Grote* believes that Demosthenes was incorrupt, and not at all visionary or unpractical in his political views. His conduct during the remainder of his life is certainly, when fairly considered, in harmony with

* Grote's Greece, vol. xii. ch. xcv., Part II.

all his previous course, and it is evident those who knew him best regarded him as a sincere patriot.⌐

That he deserved the civic triumph which he achieved in his contest with Æschines, no one who studies the two orations will fairly doubt; and it may not be out of place to present here some views upon their comparative merits.

Ingenuity, ability, and vigor of treatment, especially of the technical points of the prosecution, must be accorded to Æschines. He even rises at times to a high and sustained tone of rhetorical power. The description of the ideal patriot, the contrast between the treatment by the republic in the olden time of its public men with that of his own day, the paucity of public honors *then* bestowed with their present profusion, and the effect of each course upon the public service, the simple grandeur of the ancient worthies, the sordid huckstering for honors by the modern statesmen, and the peroration in which Solon and Aristides are heard to utter their mournful protests against the prostitution of the State's honors to unworthy men,—all these passages justify very high commendation, and must excite our admiration for the talents of the man who seems even in advance to feel the pressure of the cause he is sustaining.

But splendid as these and other parts of the oration of Æschines are, they are as nothing along-
side of the perfection of his great rival's reply.
In attempting a comparison between them we are
struck first of all with this.   There is a constraint
and artificiality with Æschines after he quits the
legal points of the prosecution.   While he divides
the public life of his rival into four parts and
pours out bitter invective upon him as to each,
there is a want of clearness and of continuity in
his treatment of the facts.   You feel, more than
once, that accusations are made on forced and improbable grounds, and that they may be, as they
seem to be, the results of private enmity and personal hostility.   Sometimes the attack is for a
matter which when fairly looked at should be the
subject of eulogy instead of dispraise, as the conduct of Demosthenes upon hearing the news of
Philip's assassination.   He is really the patriot
subduing or veiling his private sorrow, upon the
happening of an event which he believed gave
promise of relief to his oppressed country, and not
the hard-hearted man callous to all the parent's
feelings.   Again, many of the most rhetorical portions of this speech have the appearance of being
worked up and introduced for effect, instead of

flowing freely from the main current of the discourse. There is visible more of the display of
the rhetorician than the outburst of the earnest
speaker, whose words are the impassioned utterances of one who is compelled to give vent to
his pent-up feelings./ With Demosthenes all is
unforced, well arranged, faultless in method,
and, if we except the personalities indulged in,
faultless in manner. The fine description of
Philip's attempt to obtain the leadership of Greece
in spite of the injuries which Fortune had inflicted upon him follows naturally from the statement of the duty of Athens and of Demosthenes
as its counsellor to strive to maintain the high place
in Grecian affairs which the City had hitherto enjoyed. The picture of the traitors themselves betrayed and thrown aside after being used, seems
to be an essential part of the historical narrative
which is being given of the events under consideration. The matchless sublimity of the invocation
of the spirits of the men who had faced death at
Marathon and Platæa, who had fought at Salamis
and Artemisium, is necessary to the orator's argument that his country had not failed in duty
but had simply suffered from the injustice of
Fortune, and serves to point the political truth

Demosthenes had been insisting upon when he asserted that the City must have undertaken what she had, having due consideration of her real place in Greece. Everything is harmonious, easy, and consistent; and we feel that without those magnificent illustrations the lessons which are being expounded would have fallen short of their full effect, and would have failed to reach the comprehension of many who were carried away by the grandeur of the sentiments when thus presented.

That Demosthenes was master of every rhetorical resource, although abstemious in the use of ornament, is also very manifest. He never used it for its own sake it is true, but where the picture could be more completely set off by the accessories of adornment they were adopted. What more dramatic description of the consternation and paralysis which overtake a State when the unexpected tidings of disaster fall upon it, than the account of the capture of Elatea and its effect upon Athens! How truly pathetic his account of his own efforts when contrasted with the course of other orators who reserved for themselves some means of recovery in case of ultimate disaster! The apparent egotism disappears in your full persuasion, with Demosthenes himself, that he was straining every nerve to assist his country in her hour of peril. How inexpressibly touching, in the closing paragraphs of this great harangue, is his account of himself in the time of his country's adversity, when poor and broken he was still her steadfast friend! How awful the final imprecation upon the concealed enemies of the City who were fawning upon the Stranger, whilst they were belittling Athens!

It is to be remarked that Æschines oftentimes anticipates what his opponent was going to say, and endeavors to meet and answer it. Whether this is only the result of the final retouching of his speech for publication after both had been delivered, or whether the heads of each oration had been mutually exchanged beforehand, or carried from one to the other by their respective partisans, is not known. But in some instances Demosthenes makes no reference to matters which his rival speaks of in advance as being in the intended line of his reply. The reader by having the two orations side by side can the better make his own comparisons and draw his own conclusions.

The authenticity of many, indeed of most, of the documents given in the speech of Demosthenes has been denied, and it is believed upon sufficient

grounds found in the names of the archons, and the style of the pieces themselves. It is thought, however, that they should not be rejected altogether, but that their substance is probably near the truth. In the oration of Æschines we do not find the text of any of the documents cited.

ÆSCHINES

AGAINST

CTESIPHON.

ÆSCHINES AGAINST CTESIPHON.

You see, Athenians, what preparations are on foot, what forces are arrayed, what appeals to the Assembly are being made by certain persons to prevent the proper and ordinary course of justice from having its effect in the City. For myself I come before you, first, with a firm belief in the immortal Gods, next, with an abiding confidence in the laws and in you, convinced that intrigues will not more avail with you than these laws and the cause of justice.

I could indeed have fain desired that both in the Council of Five Hundred, and in the Assembly, the presiding officers had compelled conformity to established rules of debate, and that the laws had been inforced concerning the orderly deportment of public speakers which were laid down by Solon. It should thus have been permitted to the oldest citizens, as the laws prescribe, to ascend the platform decorously, and without tumult or annoyance according to their experience express their opinions upon what they regarded most advantageous to the City. Afterwards, each citizen in order of seniority should have in turn

3

presented his independent views upon every question. In this way it seems to me would the affairs of the City have been best conducted, and prosecutions have been reduced within the smallest compass. Since however the old recognized rules of procedure have been swept away, and certain men recklessly introduce illegal propositions, and certain others put them to the vote,—men who have managed to secure the presidency, not by just and proper means, but taking possession of it by contrivance,—it is brought to pass that if any other senator shall succeed in reaching the first place in due course of law and shall then attempt to obtain the result of your votes properly, such an one is denounced and impeached by the men who regard our government as no longer a common inheritance but as their own peculiar property. And when in this way by reducing private citizens to servitude and by securing absolute power to themselves they have overthrown established legal judgments, and have passed decrees according to the dictates of their passions, there shall be heard no longer that most beautiful and proper invitation of the herald, "Who desires to express his opinion, of citizens of fifty years of age and upwards, and afterwards, of all others in rotation?" Thus neither the laws, nor the senators, nor the presidents, nor the presiding tribe itself a tenth part of the City, can control the indecent conduct of these orators.

Such being the case, and such the position in which

the City is placed,—and you must be convinced that
this is so,—one part at least of the constitution, if
I know anything of the matter, still survives,—the
right of prosecution for proposing unconstitutional
measures. Should you destroy this right, or surrender it to those who will destroy it, I prophesy that
you will have unconsciously. given away to a few men
almost our entire form of government. For you must
surely know, Athenians, that but three forms of government exist, monarchy, oligarchy, and democracy:
the two former are administered according to the
feelings and opinions of those who are at the head
of affairs, but republics repose upon the authority of
law. Let no one of you therefore forget, but on the
contrary let him lay it carefully to heart, that when
he enters this tribunal for the trial of such an issue,
on that day he is called upon to cast his vote upon
his own right of free speech. Therefore was it that
our old law-givers placed in the forefront of the
juror's oath these words, "I will render a verdict according to law," knowing well that when the laws
were jealously observed by the City, free institutions
were safe.

Wherefore it is that bearing these things in mind
you should hold in abhorrence all who commit unconstitutional acts, and that you should look upon
no infraction of the constitution as small or unim-
portant, but treat all as of the gravest nature. Nor
should you suffer any man to deprive you of this

most vital right,—neither the persuasions of the generals who for a long time past have been at work
with certain of our orators to overthrow the constitution, nor the solicitations of strangers whom those
whose administration has been illegal have brought
up hither to screen them from justice; but as each
one of you would blush to quit the ranks in which
he was stationed on the day of battle, so you should
now blush at the thought of abandoning the post in
which you are placed by the laws which are to-day
the guardians of our institutions.

You must further bear in mind that your fellow-
citizens have now intrusted to your keeping the City
itself in thus confiding the constitution to your charge;
not only those of them who are here present intent
upon the course of this trial, but those also who are
necessarily absent upon their private business. If
therefore holding in due regard these your fellow-
citizens, and remembering the oaths you have sworn
and the laws you are living under, you should convict Ctesiphon for having introduced an unconstitutional bill false in terms and injurious to the City,
overturn, Athenians, such unconstitutional enact-
ments, confirm our free institutions, and punish the
men who have been advising against the law, and
against the interests both of the State and of yourselves. If in this frame of mind you listen to the
words which are about to be spoken, I well know
that your verdict will be in accordance with justice

and right, and that it will redound to the credit of yourselves and of the whole community.

I have thus far spoken about the general nature of this prosecution, and, I hope, with sufficient fairness. I now desire to speak briefly about the laws which have been passed in regard to persons who are accountable to the State, against which the decree of Ctesiphon offends.

In former times it happened that men who had exercised the highest employments and had been intrusted with the management of the public revenues, although guilty therein of the grossest corruption, would by conniving with certain orators both in the Senate and the General Assembly anticipate all examination into their accounts by means of votes of commendation and proclamations of thanks in their behalf. Not only were citizens who attempted to bring them to justice for the state of their accounts in this way much perplexed, but the jurors themselves who were to try the cause were reduced to a grave dilemma. And many of these officials, although clearly proved to have embezzled public moneys in the most flagrant way, were yet permitted to leave the judgment-seat unpunished. And not unreasonably. For the jurors were ashamed, it seems to me, that it should appear that the same man in the same City, and perchance in the very same year, who had been proclaimed in the Assemblies as worthy of being honored with a golden crown

by the people for his virtue and uprightness, should
a short time afterwards be brought to trial, and go
forth from our courts of justice convicted of fraud
in his accounts. So that the jurors were compelled,
as it were, to give their verdict not so much upon
the crime which was proven, as in regard to the
honor of the City itself. And hence it was that
one of our law-givers provided for this very emergency by propounding a law—and a most admirable
one it was—by which the coronation of all persons
liable to account was distinctly forbidden. Notwithstanding the passage of this law, evasions of it more
efficacious than the law itself have been invented, in
ignorance of which, unless they be explained to you,
you would be entirely deceived. Thus decrees for
the crowning of officials whilst they were still liable
to account were introduced contrary to law by men
not ill disposed by nature,—if any one can be well
disposed who thus acts illegally,—and by way of a
salvo to propriety they added to the propositions the
words, "after they shall have rendered a correct account of their administration." The City, however,
was injured in the same way by this evasion, since
the accounting was equally forestalled by the panegyrics and votes of crowns; and the propounder of
the decree, by thus qualifying it, admitted to his
discredit that at the time of its proposal he was con-
scious of an intended infraction of the law. But this
fellow Ctesiphon, men of Athens, at one bound clears

both law and qualification; for by his decree he asks that Demosthenes while actually in office, before he has furnished any explanations or delivered in any accounts, shall be crowned by the people.

13 Again, Athenians, they make use of another subterfuge altogether different from the one just adverted to. For they assert that an employment to which one is called under a decree is not a public charge, but a commission or agency. A public charge, they contend, is such an one only as is designated by lot by the Archons in the temple of Theseus, or such as the people themselves elect to in their assemblies; such as those of generals, commanders of cavalry, and the like: all others, they say, are but commissions injoined by virtue of a decree. To all these subtleties I oppose the law itself enacted by you with the declared intention of defeating such evasions. This law enacts in express terms that "all charges conferred by the vote of the people"—(for the framer of the law included in a single word all charges and characterized them as all such as were conferred by a vote of the people—) "and," it further says, "all persons set over public works,"—(now Demosthenes was commissioner to repair the walls, thus set over the most important of all our works,—) "all who shall handle public property for more than thirty days, and all who shall preside over a tribunal;"—(and all persons who are set over public works are entitled so to preside—.) What

then does the law direct all such to do?— To exercise their charge,—not their commission,—after having been qualified in a tribunal; since even charges conferred by lot cannot be exercised·until they have been judicially confirmed. And the law compels all such, as well as all others who exercise a public charge, to submit their accounts to the controller and the public auditors. That I have stated this accurately the laws which will now be read to you will show.

LAWS.

When therefore, Athenians, what the law calls a public charge, these men choose to call a commission, it becomes your duty to remind them of this, to oppose the law itself to their impudent construction, and to make it plain to them that you see through the vicious sophistry by which the enactment is attempted to be set aside by false glosses and evasions; and to let them feel, moreover, that the greater their ingenuity in attempting to give an illegal exposition, the greater shall be the weight of your displeasure upon them. It is right indeed, men of Athens, that the law and the public speaker should utter the self-same sound; but when the law speaks in one way, and the orator in another, it must surely be to the integrity of the law, not to the insolent assertions of its opponent, that every suffrage should be given.

I wish here to reply briefly to an argument which

Demosthenes regards as impregnable. "I am," says he, "a member of the Walls Commission. I admit it. But I have given one hundred minæ of my own money towards the better construction of the work. For what then am I accountable, unless private liberality is to be the subject of public accountability?" Listen to my just and proper answer to this piece of sophistry.

In this ancient City of ours, so vast in its extent, no one has ever been exempted from accountability for any employment whatsoever undertaken in the public service. The examples which I shall first refer to may doubtless surprise you, for I shall now mention the ministers of religion of both sexes, who receive merely honorary compensation, and whose duty is confined to putting up prayers to the deities in your behalf. These are all accountable both collectively and individually;—not only in particular, but whole families in common, the Eumolpidæ and the Kerykes, and all others. Again, trierarchs are accountable by law, although they have not handled public money, nor diverted from you large portions of your revenues whilst they have expended but a trifle, neither found asserting they have given to you of their own whilst they have been but returning what belonged to you; and this, too, when by the admission of all they have been consuming their own patrimony in the expression of their good-will to the State. And not only the trierarchs, but our most important assemblies are bound to submit to the judgment of the State tribunals.

First of all, the law requires the Council of the Areopagus to give an account of its transactions and to submit its proceedings to examination by the State officials; and this august tribunal which deals with the largest affairs is thus brought under your control. Shall it be said then that this Council shall never be crowned?—Certainly, for it is not allowed by their ancient constitution.—Are they then insensible to honor?—So far from this, that, not content with interdicting to themselves every species of injustice, they even punish the slightest fault committed by their members; whilst your orators insolently hold themselves above the law itself. Again, your law-givers have made the Council of Five Hundred accountable: and so resolute is its distrust of all officials thus made liable, that at the head of the law itself is inscribed "that no magistrate who may be called upon to account shall absent himself from the City."—"By Hercules," shall some one then exclaim, "because I have exercised a public charge, shall I not leave the country when I will?"—"No, you cannot, lest in your flight you carry off with you the property or the secrets of the State."—

Furthermore, the law permits not that one liable to account shall consecrate his estate to religion, or make offerings to the Gods, or become adopted, or make a testamentary disposition, or commit many

other acts. In a word, the law holds in pledge each
official's entire estate, until he shall have rendered to
the State the most absolute account of his transactions
with it. Is there none then in the public service who
may not have disbursed public money, or even handled it when in office?—Even such an one the law
directs to account before the Auditors.—How then
shall he do this, when he has neither received nor
spent the public money?—The law gives the answer,
and tells us what such an one shall say; for it orders
him to declare even so,—" I have neither touched
nor spent the moneys of the City."—Nothing then
throughout the State is exempt from the duty of accounting, or from inquiry, or from investigation.—
That I speak truth in this matter hear from the laws
themselves.

LAWS.

When Demosthenes shall therefore with triumphant
air boldly assert that he is not accountable for what
he gave, answer him thus: " Should you not, Demosthenes, have permitted the herald of the public
auditors to proclaim in ancient and fitting form, ' who
wishes to accuse?' Suffer it to be objected to you by
any one who wishes, that you have given nothing,
but after having received from the City ten talents
for the purpose, you have out of this large sum spent
but a little upon the reparation of the walls. Clutch
not by force these civic honors, nor snatch their suffrages from the judges' hands. Hold yourself under,

not above the law; for thus are our democratic institutions upheld."

Such, then, is my answer to the frivolous pretexts which my adversaries have hitherto opposed to me. I shall now attempt to prove to you from the public records that when Ctesiphon proposed his decree, Demosthenes was really accountable, as he was at that time Administrator of the Theoric Fund and also Superintendent of Repairs of Walls, and had not yet rendered any account of his management of these employments. Let the Clerk now read in whose archonship, and in what month and on what day, and in what Assembly, Demosthenes was elected to administer the Theoric Fund.

ENUMERATION OF DATES.

If therefore I go no further than I have done, Ctesiphon will stand justly convicted, for he is condemned not by my charge, but by the public records.

In days of yore, Athenians, there was a controller chosen by the people who in each presidency accounted to it for the public revenues. By reason of the confidence which had been reposed in Eubulus, the men who (before the law of Hegemon) were chosen to administer the Theoric Fund exercised at the same time the offices of controller, of receiver-general, of superintendent of marine, and of inspector of arsenals. They were also intrusted with the repair of the highways, and controlled in effect almost the

—27.]

tire municipal govern...
or blaming any one
how you that the law-...
f these functionaries
rendered correct accou...
Ctesiphon, however, has
decree for the crowning
single person united all
of Athens.

To prove that when Ctesiphon brough...
cree, his friend was also Superintendent
of Walls, was handling the Public mone...
posing fines like other magistrates, and w...
in tribunals, I shall produce to you the t...
Demosthenes and Ctesiphon themselves.
archonship of Chærondas, on the twenty...
of the month Thargelion, Demosthenes i...
-bly of the people brought forward a d...
assembling of the tribes upon the seco...
days of the month Scirophorion; and a...
decree he proposed, that from every tri...
selected persons to oversee the Work up...
and to regulate the expenditure for it...
properly too;—in order that the City...
responsible citizens to whom to look fo...
f these outlays.

DECREES.

Yea, but in the face of all this, Demosthenes insists that he did not become Superintendent of Repairs of Walls, either by lot, or by the votes of the people. And on this both he and Ctesiphon will dilate. My answer shall be short and clear, and shall pierce through all their sophistries. I wish first, however, to make a few general remarks upon the subject.

There are three kinds of magistracies, Athenians; of which the first and most obvious class is that which is either chosen by lot or elected by the people; the next is composed of those who handle public money for over thirty days, or who are set over public works; the third class is designated by law to include "all who may be otherwise chosen and who preside over tribunals, and who must be confirmed before they exercise their charge." Thus, after excluding magistrates chosen by the people or by lot, there remains the class of functionaries chosen by the tribes, or by the thirds, or by the demes, from their own bodies to administer public funds; and this occurs when, as in this instance, the tribes are charged with the duty of digging trenches, or of constructing galleys. The truth of what I advance will be manifest from the laws themselves.

LAWS.

Bear in mind, then, what has just been said, that the law directs those who have been selected from the body of the tribes to be first judicially approved. Now the tribe Pandíon has chosen Demosthenes to the office of Superintendent of Repairs of Walls, and he has received from the Treasury for this purpose nearly ten talents. Another law forbids the honoring of a magistrate with a crown while still accountable; and you are sworn to give your verdict according to law. But Ctesiphon has introduced a decree for the crowning of an accountable magistrate, without even adding the words, "after he shall have rendered his accounts." I expose its illegality, and I support my charge by the laws, the decrees, by my adversaries themselves. How then can you have a plainer case of violation of law by the introduction of an illegal decree?

I shall now demonstrate to you that the decree is also illegal in providing as it does for the proclamation of the crown. The law directs explicitly that if the crown be conferred by the Senate, it shall be proclaimed in the Senate Chamber, if by the People, in the Assembly, and in no other place. Read the law.

LAW.

And the law, Athenians, wisely thus provides. For the legislature, I fancy, deemed it improper that a public man should be honored before strangers, but that he should content himself with a distinction from the hands of his own people in the City itself, and that he should never trade for self-advancement

4

in the proclamation of a public honor.—Thus thought
indeed the law-giver; but how thought Ctesiphon?
Read the decree.

DECREE.

You have just heard, Athenians, that the law
directs the proclamation of one who is crowned by
the people to be made in the Pnyx at an Assembly
of the people, and nowhere else. Ctesiphon however
not only transgresses the law by directing it to be
done in the theatre, thus changing the place from
that where the Athenians hold their Assembly, but
he commands it to take place not before the people
alone, but in presence of the assembled Greeks, that
they may see along with us what manner of man it is
whom we thus honor.

The framer of this decree having thus then plainly
violated the law shall be now seen arrayed with Demosthenes in raising up subtleties to defeat it. That
you may not be deceived through ignorance of them,
I will expose and exhibit them in advance. These
men will not indeed assert that the laws do not forbid the proclamation of one who is crowned by the
people to be made outside of an Assembly of the people, but they will bring in as their justification a law
concerning the Dionysiac festivals; and making use
of only a portion of it, they will practise upon your
discernment, by laying before you an enactment
which has no application to the present prosecution.
They will tell you that there are two laws in our

City relative to proclamations: one, which I have just presented, which indeed expressly forbids a citizen who is crowned by the people from being so proclaimed outside of an Assembly; another quite opposite, which authorizes the proclamation to be made in the theatre at the representation of the tragedies, provided the people shall so direct. And under this last-named law they will assert that Ctesiphon wrote his decree.

Against this artifice I present the laws themselves as advocates, as I shall earnestly and persistently continue to do throughout this whole controversy. If such a thing could indeed be true, and such a practice could have crept into your polity as to leave laws without force standing along with laws in full force, and two laws directly contradictory could be found side by side relating to the same subject, what should be said of a government in which the law injoins at one and the same time to do and not to do the same act? But it is not so, and may you never fall into such a disorder of the law! The founders of our popular constitution were not unmindful of such a contingency, and have expressly injoined upon the junior archons to propose every year to the people a reformation of the laws, after making a careful examination as to whether any enactment exists at variance with any other, or whether repealed laws are found among those in force, or whether there are redundant or pleonastic statutes. And should any

such be found, the junior archons are directed to
have them inscribed and attached to the statues of
our heroes for inspection; and the senators are then
required to call an Assembly of the people, and to lay
before them the names of their propounders. The
president is then to take the vote of the people upon
the question of which laws shall be abrogated and
which shall continue operative, so that there shall be
finally found but a single enactment in force upon
the same subject.

Read here the laws.

LAWS.

If then, Athenians, the assertion of these men
were true, and there had been two laws in existence
upon the subject of proclamations, it seems plain to
me that the archons would have discovered them
and the presidents would have returned them to their
propounders; and one or other of them, either that
which gave authority to make the proclamation or
that which withheld it, would have been repealed.
But since none of these things has taken place, they
are plainly convicted not only of advancing a wilful
untruth but an impossibility. I shall now expose
to you the source from which they draw this falsehood in explaining the origin of the laws relating to
proclamations in the theatre.

At the season of the new tragedies, certain citizens
without having obtained authority from the people

would cause themselves to be proclaimed, some as being crowned by their tribesmen, others by their fellows of the deme; nay, there would be others who having ordered silence to be proclaimed by the herald would publicly manumit their slaves, calling upon all Greece to witness their enfranchisement. But what was even more disgusting, certain citizens who had found means to enter into relations of hospitality with foreign cities, would actually cause it to be then proclaimed, that they had been honored with a crown on account of their virtue and valor by the citizens, for instance, of Rhodes, or of Chios, or of any other city. And this they did, not after having first obtained your consent, for which they would have been your debtors for at least thanks, as citizens who are crowned by the Senate or by the People, but upon their own decision, without any decree at all. In consequence of this the spectators, the chorus-masters and the actors were much annoyed; and the men who were proclaimed in this way in the theatre really received a higher honor than citizens who were crowned by the people. For to these last a place, namely the Assembly, was designated, in which they should be crowned, and it was interdicted to them to be proclaimed elsewhere; whereas the others were proclaimed in the presence of all Greece:—the former, at your instance, by authority of a decree;—the latter, without any decree at all.

In view of this abuse, one of our legislators introduced a law which had no connection whatsoever
with the law in regard to the crowning by the people,
and which of course in no wise affected it; since it
was not the Assembly of the people, but the representations at the theatre which were interfered with by
the course which had been pursued. And the new
enactment did not clash with existing laws,—for that
was not permissible,—but it operated simply upon
such persons as were crowned without a decree by
the tribes and demes, and upon citizens who enfranchised their slaves, and upon crowns voted by foreign
cities. It expressly forbade the manumission of a
slave in the theatre, or the proclamation of a crown
conferred by the tribes or demes, or by any one else,
under pain of infamy to the herald.

Since then it is directed that those honored with a
crown by the Senate shall be proclaimed in the Senate Chamber, and those crowned by the people in the
Assembly, and it is interdicted to those crowned by
the tribes or demes to be so proclaimed in the theatre,
that no one by mean solicitations for crowns and
proclamations should thereby obtain a spurious
honor, and it is moreover forbidden by the law that
proclamation shall be made by any one unless by the
Senate, the people, the tribes and the demes; if all
these be excepted, what remains but the case of crowns
conferred by foreign states? That this is manifestly
so, I shall convince you by the laws themselves.

/ Besides it is injoined by law that the crown of gold which shall be proclaimed in the theatre in behalf of any one shall be taken from him and consecrated to Athene. Who would dare however from this to accuse the people of Athens of a sordid economy? Never was there a city, never an individual, so destitute of generosity, as in the same moment to proclaim, take away, and consecrate a crown of their own bestowal!/ This consecration is doubtless directed to be made because the crown has been conferred by strangers, that no man may estimate a foreign honor as of greater value than his country, and may not be tempted in consequence to fail in his devotion to her. The crown conferred by the people and proclaimed in the Assembly is never consecrated, but on the contrary is permitted to be enjoyed not only by its recipient but by his descendants, that by preserving this memorial in their family they may never become ill-disposed to their country. And this is the reason why the law-maker has prohibited the proclamation in the theatre of a crown conferred by strangers unless authorized by a decree of the people;—that the foreign city which may desire so to honor one of your citizens shall first through an embassy demand it of the people; and thus he who is crowned shall owe a higher debt of gratitude to you who have permitted the proclamation than to those who have presented him with the crown itself. Let the laws be read in proof of my assertion.

LAWS.

When therefore these men in the desire of deceiving you shall cry out that the law allows the crowning to take place in the theatre if the people so decree, remember to answer them thus:—"Yes, if it be a crown conferred by another city. But if it be the Athenian people which gives it, the place in which it is to be done is absolutely settled: it is unlawful to proclaim it outside of an Assembly. Should you spend the whole day in twisting the words, 'and never elsewhere,' you shall fail to show that your decree was in conformity to the law."

There remains to be considered a part of the prosecution upon which I shall dwell with great earnestness:—the pretext by which Demosthenes is asserted to be worthy of the honor of the crown. The decree in question alleges in this respect "that the herald shall proclaim in the theatre to the Greeks that the Athenian people crowns Demosthenes for his virtue and probity," and, above all, "for his persevering efforts both by speech and action to achieve the best results for his country." My argument on this point shall be simple and easily understood by you who are to pass upon the question. As prosecutor it is my duty to establish that this commendation of Demosthenes is utterly false, because he has never been found nor is he now found advising or doing the best for his country. If I show this, Ctesiphon must

be undoubtedly fairly convicted, since all our laws
forbid the introduction of falsehood into the public
records. The defendant to insure his acquittal must
establish the opposite of this: and you will decide
upon the strength of our arguments and assertions.
Such then is the state of the case. *ll-)l*

To pass in review the whole life of Demosthenes
would occupy too much time, and of what profit to
us would it be to discuss it? It would be of no value
to speak of the prosecution brought by him for his
wound before the Council of Areopagus against his
relative Demomeles the Pæanian, and to tell of the
gashes he inflicted upon his own head. Nor need I
speak of the expedition of Kephisodotus when he
sailed with the fleet to the Hellespont, Demosthenes
as one of the trierarchs having the admiral in his
own ship, eating at the same table with him, sharing
in his libations and sacrifices, and asserting a claim
to this intimacy by reason of a family friendship, and
yet not hesitating to denounce him and to become
his accuser in a case of life and death. Or why
should I refer to the affair with Midias and the blows
which Demosthenes received from him in the theatre
when he was exercising his duties as chorus-master,
and how he compounded for thirty minæ the outrage
against himself and the judgment which the people
had pronounced against Midias in the temple of Dionysus? I ought, it seems to me, to pass over all
such details; not in the desire of either deceiving

you, or of betraying my cause, but in the apprehension that I might incur your displeasure in the recital of facts confessedly true indeed, but stale and known to every one. And you, Ctesiphon, I ask, which is the most proper treatment for a man whose baseness is so familiar and clear to the hearers, that his accuser is compelled to omit charges not because they are untrue but only too old and notorious? Is it right that such an one should be honored with a crown of gold, or rather be branded with infamy? You who have insolently dared to introduce falsehoods into a decree, shall you brave our halls of justice with impunity, or shall punishment be inflicted upon you by the City?

In regard to Demosthenes's public offences, I shall endeavor to speak more directly. I understand that he intends, when it comes to his turn to address you, to divide into periods the time of his public career. The first of these, as I am informed, he dates from our war with Philip about Amphipolis, and concludes with the peace and alliance brought about by Philocrates of Agnusia with his own assistance, as I shall plainly prove to you. The next he will fix as including the period of the peace until the day when this same orator caused it to be broken by his declaration of war. The third covers the period of the war until the fatal day of Chæronea: and the fourth will bring us thence to the present time. He has thus, as I hear, divided his whole administration, and he intends, it seems, to demand of me as to which of the four periods I accuse him, and when it was that I charge him with not having well served his country; and he proclaims that should I refuse to answer and should I wrap myself up in my robe and try to escape, he will strip me bare, and drag me to the tribunal where he will force me to speech. That he may not then insolently prevail, and that you may be forewarned, and that I may reply, I now say to you, Demosthenes, in presence of all the jurors, and the other citizens who are standing round us, in presence of the assembled Greeks who have thought fit to be here during this trial, (I see them not a few, but in numbers vastly greater than any one can remember to have ever beheld at a public prosecution,) I answer that I accuse you in regard to each and every one of the four periods which you have thought fit to name. And with the permission of the Gods, and an impartial hearing from the jurors, if I am only able to recollect what I know in regard to you, I shall make it clear as day that to the Divinity and to those who have conducted our affairs with propriety and moderation is it that the City owes to-day the security she enjoys; while you, Demosthenes, shall be proved to have been the author of all the calamities she has undergone. I shall adopt the same order and division which I am told he will use, and will first refer to the first period, next to the second, thirdly to that which succeeded it, and finally discuss our present situation. And I shall direct myself in the outset to the peace which was engineered by you and Philocrates.

It was in your power, men of Athens, to have made the first peace with the consent of the General Assembly of the Greeks, had certain of your public men suffered you to await the return of the embassies which you had sent at that time to the different States, inviting them to unite in a general Grecian Confederacy against Philip; for it was a period favorable to the recovery of our ascendency with the consent of the Greeks. This advantage you lost through the corruption of Demosthenes and Philocrates, who were purchased to conspire against the public interests. Should this statement falling suddenly upon your ears strike any of you as improbable, hearken attentively to what I am about to say, just as we do when we sit down to examine an old account of expenditures. We sometimes undoubtedly leave home with false opinions in regard to our accounts; yet when the reckoning has been made, none is so unreasonable as not to assent to and recognize the correctness of what the calculation has proved. And so should you now listen to what I am about to say. Should any of you have come from home in the long-entertained belief that Demosthenes could never have urged Philip's interests in concert with Philocrates, let him, I say, who is so disposed suspend his judgment until after he hears me:—for this is only justice. If you give me your attention then while I briefly recall to you these periods, if I show you the very decree proposed by Demosthenes in conjunction with Philocrates, if an examination into the truth of the matter convicts him of having written more decrees than his confederate in the first negotiations about the peace and the alliance, of having flattered Philip to the depths of baseness, of having refused to wait the return of our envoys, and of having prevented our people from concluding the peace with the Common Assembly of the Greeks, of having delivered up to Philip Kersobleptes king of Thrace the friend and ally of Athens;—if I demonstrate all this, I claim of you this moderate favor :— concede to me, in the name of Heaven, that this man in the first of these four periods at least did not well administer our affairs.—I shall expose all this so that you may readily follow me.

Philocrates had proposed a decree by which Philip should be allowed to send hither a herald and ambassadors to treat of peace. This was attacked as contrary to law ; a day was fixed for the trial ; Lykinus prosecuted, Philocrates defended himself and was supported by Demosthenes, and acquitted. Then came the time when Themistocles was archon. Without a title either by original selection or as substitute for another, but brought in through bribery and intrigue, Demosthenes became a senator, that in the Senate he might uphold Philocrates both by word

and deed, as the result has clearly shown. For Philocrates was thus enabled to obtain the passage of
another decree by which the deputies were directed
to be chosen to proceed to Philip to ask him to
send hither plenipotentiaries to negotiate a peace.
Amongst the number of deputies Demosthenes was
found, and upon his return from Macedon he spoke
strongly in favor of peace, and confirmed the report
of the other deputies. Alone of all the Senate he
proposed to conclude a treaty with Philip's herald
and ambassadors, conforming in all this to the views
of Philocrates. The one obtained authority for
Philip's herald and envoys to be sent hither; the
other closed with them after their arrival. For what
followed, give me here your most earnest attention.

The negotiations were carried on by Demosthenes
and Philocrates alone without the other deputies, who
upon this change of affairs were shortly afterwards
grossly calumniated by Demosthenes; and this was
not surprising, as these two men had been joined in
the embassy and had prepared the decrees in concert.
And by these decrees, first, they brought it to pass
that you should refuse to await the return of the envoys who had been sent by you to stir up the Greeks
against Philip, in order that you might conclude
peace with him separately, and without the other
Greeks. Next, you were induced not only to make
peace with Philip, but to enter into an alliance with
him, so that your partisans in the other States might

be reduced to despair when they saw you urging
them to war with Philip, and at the same time not
only concluding peace with him at Athens but entering into a strict alliance with him. Lastly, Kersobleptes king of Thrace was not only not included in
this convention, but was not permitted to participate
either in the peace or the alliance; although the
expedition was actually then on foot against him.

The king of Macedon indeed who had purchased
these advantages was not acting unfairly in this
matter, since he had a right to obtain what was best
for himself before taking the oaths and entering
into the treaties; but these men who were betraying and selling out to him the resources of the
State deserved your hottest indignation. And yet
this Demosthenes who is telling us he is now the
enemy of Alexander as he then was of Philip, while
he is reproaching me with the friendship of the
former, snatched from you the time for consideration, by directing the presidents to call an Assembly
of the people upon the eighth day of Elaphebolion,
a holiday consecrated to the games and sacrifices of
Esculapius,—a thing theretofore unheard of. And
what was his excuse for this? Why, forsooth, that
when Philip's deputies should arrive, you could deliberate without delay upon his propositions. He
thus procured in advance an Assembly for deputies
who were still in Macedonia, deprived you of the
opportunity for discussion, and hurried through the

whole matter in order that you might conclude peace
by yourselves, in the absence of your deputies, and
without the concurrence of the other Greeks.   Meanwhile Philip's deputies arrived, while yours who were
exciting the other Greeks against him were still away.
Then it was that Demosthenes pushed through another decree, by which, without waiting for your own
envoys, you were to deliberate on the instant immediately after the Dionysiac festivals on the eighteenth
and nineteenth of the month, not only upon the peace
but upon the alliance with the king of Macedon.
For the truth of this I appeal to the decree.

The Assemblies were accordingly convened, after
these festivals had been celebrated; and upon the
first of them a common resolve of the Allies was
read, the heads of which I will now briefly state.
And first they desired that you should deliberate in
regard to the peace separately, omitting all reference
to the alliance, not from forgetfulness, but because
they thought that even the peace itself was more
necessary than honorable.   Next, in the endeavor to
provide against the corruption of Demosthenes they
inserted in the resolve that to any of the Grecian
States it should be permitted during the space of
three months to be inscribed upon the same pillar
with the Athenians and thus to participate with
them in the same stipulations and treaties.

Two important advantages were thus secured: first,
a gain of three months' time for the preparation of

the Grecian Embassies; secondly, the obtaining for Athens of the good-will of the other Greeks through a General Assembly: so that if the treaty were violated we should not be compelled to fight alone and unsupported, in which condition we have been placed through the mismanagement of Demosthenes. The reading of these documents will establish the correctness of my statements.

THE RESOLUTIONS OF THE ALLIES.

I declared myself, I now avow, in favor of this resolution, as did all who spoke in this first Assembly. And the people went away in the conviction that peace should be concluded, but that it was inexpedient to deliberate at that time about the alliance, in consequence of the invitation from the other Greeks; but that it should be engaged in in conjunction with the rest of Greece. Night intervened. The **next** day we reassembled; and then Demosthenes getting possession of the platform, to the exclusion of every one else, proclaimed that the discussion of the day before was utterly worthless, unless Philip's deputies would consent to such an arrangement. And he asserted that he knew not of any peace separate from the alliance. "It will not do," said he,—(I remember well his expression from my repugnance both to the speaker and his words,—) "it will not do to sever the alliance from the peace, nor to wait upon the delays of the other Greeks.

We must either fight alone, or conclude a separate peace." When he had ended, he called Antipater to the platform, and put some questions to him, having concerted with him in advance both the questions to be asked and the answers to be given to them against the City's interests. In the end this course prevailed, Demosthenes carrying his point by words, and Philocrates embodying them in the decree.

There still remained to be effected by them the betrayal of Kersobleptes with the kingdom of Thrace. This was accomplished upon the 26th of the same Elaphebolion, before Demosthenes set out upon his last embassy to receive the oaths. Yes! this orator who now proclaims himself before you as such an enemy of Philip and of Alexander, who orders you to load down the Macedonians with abuse, went twice as ambassador to Macedon, when there was no need for him even to go at all. This senator through intrigue, sitting then in this Assembly of the 26th, surrendered Kersobleptes in concert with Philocrates. For Philocrates caused to be secretly inserted in the decree a clause which Demosthenes procured to be carried with the others, "that the representatives of the allies should on that very day exchange oaths with Philip's deputies." But as no representative of Kersobleptes was present, a decree which compelled the deputies then present to exchange oaths, in effect excluded Kersobleptes who was absent.

THE DECREE. THE PRESIDENT.

Admirable indeed, Athenians, admirable is the provision by which our public records are preserved forever! Immutable, and changing not with the shifting opinions of the political renegades who readily pass from one side to the other, they hold up before the eyes of the people a certain means of information whenever it chooses to look into the antecedents of the faithless men who pretend to have become all at once upright citizens! And it will be well for me to exhibit just here an instance of this fellow's sycophancy. During the year of his senatorship he appears to have not once moved that the ambassadors from any other country should receive the honor of precedency. But now for the first and only time he accords to Philip's envoys the highest place of honor. He orders cushions to be brought for them to repose upon, has tapestry spread around them, and at the dawn of day conducts them to the theatre with such unseemly flattery, that he is greeted with hisses from the people for his abject adulation towards them. When the envoys set out for Thebes on their return, they were conducted thither in three carriages drawn by mules hired expressly by Demosthenes, who thus held up his City to be the laughing-stock of Greece. That I may pause for a moment on this subject, let the clerk read here the decree in regard to the precedence awarded to the ambassadors.

DECREE.

And yet this gross, this abject flatterer, Athenians, when he obtained, through the spies sent to him by Charidemus, the first intelligence of Philip's assassination, falsely asserted that he had not so learnt it from Charidemus, but from the Gods themselves in a vision, which he forged for the occasion. Yes, this man who by day outrages the divinities by his perjured appeals to them, has, he asserts, communications by night from Jupiter and from Athene, in which they reveal to him what is to take place in the future! On the seventh day from his daughter's death, before he had even mourned for her, or accomplished the last rites of affection, he comes forth in public, crowned with a garland of flowers, and in a white robe, and offers up sacrifices to the Gods for the deliverance;—the unnatural wretch thus acting in defiance of the laws of decency, the parent who had just lost her who was the first and only one who ever called him by the name of father! I wish not to insult his misfortune, but I choose to display his real character. The unfeeling parent, the bad father, can never become the upright statesman. He who cherishes and loves not those who are bound to him by the dearest and nearest ties, will never exhibit a stronger attachment to you who are strangers to him. The wicked man in private life will never prove the virtuous counsellor towards the public;—and he who is shewn to have been heartless and worthless in his own home was never the good and upright representative of Athens in Macedonia :—he had only changed his country, not his nature.

We now approach the second period to which I have referred; and here we may well ask how it was that while Philocrates was denounced and driven into exile for the same political acts which he had committed along with Demosthenes, the latter stepped forth as the accuser of others, and, corrupt as he was, was enabled to plunge us into our present miseries?

When Philip had suddenly passed Thermopylæ, and contrary to all expectation had destroyed the cities of the Phocians, raising up the power of the Thebans, as you then thought, to a height which threatened the general advantage of Greece as well as your particular interests, in alarm and dismay you hurried in all your effects from the country, and the deputies who had been concerned in the embassy for the peace were bitterly denounced by you. Philocrates and Demosthenes were censured above all others, because, besides being of the embassy, they had introduced the decrees. At this moment the two men were at variance, quarrelling perhaps about matters which you may readily suspect. Seeing the storm impending, and taking counsel from the innate depravity of his heart, and filled with a mean jealousy of Philocrates in regard to the wages of his venality, Demosthenes resolved upon his course. He thought

that if he now appeared as the accuser of his fellow-
ambassadors, and attacked Philip himself, Philocrates would be lost, his colleagues in danger, and
himself raised to the highest point of esteem for thus
wickedly betraying his friends under the guise of
fidelity to the public cause. The factious and tur-
bulent citizens, seeing this, readily seconded him by
calling him to the platform, and proclaimed him as
the one incorruptible public man. He acquiesced in
their views, and thus furnished them with the be-
ginnings of war and confusion. This is the man,
Athenians, who first found out about the strong
place Serrium, and Doriscum, and Ergiske, and
Murgiske, and Garros, and Ganida, places the very
names of which were up to this time unknown to us.
And he carried matters to such a point that if Philip
did not send us his ambassadors, he said he was
treating the City with disrespect;—if he sent them,
he called them spies, not ambassadors. Did Philip
desire to refer the decision of our disputes to the
umpirage of some fair and impartial people, he asserted none could be found to adjudge equitably between us and the king of Macedon. When this
prince gave up Halonesus to us, Demosthenes forbade us to receive it;—he should *restore* it, not *give* it,
he said, thus disputing about terms. And finally,
by causing a crown to be conferred upon those who
under the leadership of Aristodemus had gone upon
the expedition to Thessaly and Magnesia contrary to

the stipulations of our convention, he broke up the peace, and dragged his country into all the horrors of war.

True, but he tells us by the alliance of the Eubœans and of the Thebans he has surrounded our country with walls of adamant. But, men of Athens, in these very matters, although you were kept in the most profound ignorance of it, you have been most grossly wronged in three important particulars. Anxious as I am to hasten on to speak of this wonderful alliance with the Thebans, I must begin, that I may proceed in due order, with the Eubœans.

You had been treated with great injustice on many occasions not only originally by Mnesarchus of Chalcis the father of Callias and Taurosthenes, the two men whom Demosthenes has now dared for a bribe to enroll among our citizens, but more recently by Themison the Eretrian, who in time of peace robbed us of Oropus. Nevertheless when the Thebans in their descent upon the island successfully attempted to reduce their cities to subjection, forgetting your former wrongs you came willingly to their assistance, and in five days relieved them with your fleet and with an army; and before thirty days had passed having become masters of Eubœa you forced the Thebans to capitulate and retire. From a sense of honor and equity you restored the captured cities and their governments to those who had confided in you, thinking it to be beneath your character for justice to recall your animosity against a people who had relied upon your good faith.

For these enormous benefits the Chalcidians made you a poor requital. When you returned to Eubœa to assist Plutarch, they at first pretended to be your friends; but scarcely had you arrived at Tamynæ, after passing Mount Cotylus, than this same Callias whom Demosthenes had been hired to eulogize, seeing our army entangled in the defiles,—with no chance of retreat except through victory,—without hope of succor either by land or by sea,—gathered together an army throughout Eubœa which he reinforced by troops from Philip. At the same time Taurosthenes, who now extends to all of us the right hand of fellowship with a gracious smile, collected his Phocian mercenaries, and uniting with his brother, both advanced together against us for our destruction. Had not some benignant deity intervened in your behalf, and had not your soldiers, both foot and horse, performed prodigies of valor, thus enabling you to gain a pitched battle at Tamynæ near the hippodrome, where you routed and received the surrender of the enemy, the State had been in imminent danger of a most dishonorable defeat. For ill-success in war is by no means the greatest disaster which can happen; the defeat is double which is sustained in a conflict with an unworthy foe.—But in spite of all this ill-treatment from them, you were again reconciled to the Eubœans.

Callias, who had obtained your pardon, soon re-
lapsed into his original nature. Aspiring to a distinguished tyranny, he assembled in form a general
council of Eubœa at Chalcis, with the real design of
uniting the whole island against you; and in the hope
of making Philip an instrument of this movement,
he visited Macedon. There he followed that prince
up and down the country, and ranged himself in the
body of his courtiers; but having offended him he
was obliged to fly his kingdom, and he then offered
himself to the Thebans. He soon abandoned them
also, and after exhibiting more windings than the
Euripus on the banks of which he dwelt, he found
himself involved in the enmity of both the Thebans
and of Philip. In this embarrassment, uncertain
whither to turn, and an expedition being already
announced against him, he saw his only hope of
safety in persuading the Athenians to become his
allies, and to pledge themselves to his assistance
should he be attacked, which was clearly manifest
unless you interfered to prevent it.

Such being his resolve, he sent hither his deputies
Glauketes, Empedon, and that famous runner Diodo-
rus, to bear empty promises to the people, but full
purses to Demosthenes and his fellows. He purchased through them three separate advantages at
the same time. First, that he should not fail in
securing your alliance; for should you in the remembrance of his former misdeeds refuse it, no middle

course was open to him;—he must either flee from
Chalcis, or be captured and probably put to death, so
great were the forces of Philip and of the Thebans
which were arrayed against him. Next, he offered
his money freely to him who after obtaining for him
the alliance should get the City to dispense with the
necessity of the Chalcidians attending the convention
which was to sit at Athens. Lastly, that the Chalcidians should be relieved ᵥfrom all contributions.
Callias succeeded in all these projects. For Demosthenes the tyrant-hater, as he now pretends to be,
and who Ctesiphon asserts has ever counselled best
for the City, abandoned all her interests, and obtained
the making of an alliance by which we engaged to
come to the relief of the Chalcidians, getting in exchange for our services the euphemistic statement
that in case we should ever be attacked by any one,
we should be aided in turn by them. He however
surrendered altogether the sending hither of deputies
to a common assembly, as well as the furnishing of
the sinews of war in the shape of contributions; and
dignifying his abominable conduct with fine phrases,
he persuaded you that the City should first send
assistance to those Greeks who needed it, and not
concern itself about alliances until after they had
been saved. That you may be convinced of the
truth of my statements, let the decree of Callias and
the alliance be now read.

DECREE.

Disgraceful however as was this sale by Demosthenes of these splendid opportunities of the City, this abandonment of the Assemblies and of all contributions to her, what I am about to relate will strike you as still more monstrous. Callias the Chalcidian had now reached this height of effrontery and greed, and Demosthenes the hero of Ctesiphon's panegyrics sustained him in it by his venality, that in your presence and under your very eyes, they snatched from you the contributions of Oreum and Eretria, amounting to ten talents, and after having excused the deputies of those cities from coming to Athens, they reconvoked them at Chalcis at a so-called Eubœan Assembly. It is well worth hearing how and by what misfeasances they accomplished this purpose.

No longer sending hither his emissaries, Callias now presented himself in person in our Assembly, and harangued us in a speech prepared for him by Demosthenes. He told us he had just arrived from Peloponnesus where he had obtained an imposition for a fund of one hundred talents to be used against Philip, and he specified the sums to be contributed by each people. The Achæans and Megarians were to supply sixty talents and the cities of Eubœa forty, by means of which a naval and a land armament were to be secured. Many of the other Greeks would swell this contribution, so that neither money nor troops would fail. All this was plain enough, he said, but there were secret negotiations to be entered into to which some of your citizens were privy; and he wound up by calling upon Demosthenes to vouch for the truth of his assertions.

Demosthenes coming forward with an important air, began by praising Callias, and pretending to be in the secret; but he desired first, he said, to give you an account of his mission to the Peloponnesus and to Acarnania. The substance of his statement was that all the Peloponnesians and Acarnanians had been induced by him to contribute to the war against Philip; the subsidies would provide for one hundred swift-sailing vessels, ten thousand foot soldiers, and one thousand horse; and over and above this, Peloponnesus and Acarnania would each supply more than two thousand heavy-armed troops, and the command of the whole would be conferred by them upon you. The execution of this project was not to be delayed beyond the sixteenth of the month Anthesterion, for he had concerted, in these cities, for a general rendezvous at Athens on the day of the full moon.—This man has in fact a wonderful way of his own. Other impostors when they intend to deceive deal in vague and ambiguous generalities, in the fear of being called upon for proofs. But Demosthenes when he goes about to trick, first solemnly swears to the falsehood, calling down ruin upon his head with imprecations in case he forswears himself, and then confidently states propositions which he well knows can never be performed, and gives the names of persons whom he has never seen, amusing his audience by a well-feigned imitation of a truthful man. And for this especially is it that he should be held in detestation by you, for he cheats and corrupts with all the semblance of honesty itself.—

Having said all this, Demosthenes hands the clerk to read a decree longer than the Iliad, emptier than his own harangues and his own hollow life, and stuffed with hopes doomed to be disappointed, and with armies never to be levied. Having thus diverted your attention from his knavery, and kept you in suspense by these false hopes, he collects all his forces for his purpose, and writes the decree for the choice of deputies to Eretria who are to beseech the Eretrians (they must now indeed be besought) to pay their contribution of five talents not to you but to Callias. At the same time other deputies were chosen to Oreum who were to beg that people to regard as friends and enemies the friends and enemies of Athens. Then the whole trick was consummated by his causing it to be written in the decree, that the deputies should further ask the people of Oreum to pay their five talents to Callias, not to you. That all this may be manifest, take here the decree itself, strip it of all the pomp and imposture of armies and

galleys, and come to the very point of the fraudulent
advantage which this impure, this profane wretch
was here secretly appropriating to himself:—the
man who Ctesiphon declares by his decree has persevered in serving for the best the people of Athens
both by word and deed.

DECREE.

You thus got fine words about galleys, armies,
the full moon, and general assemblies, but in deed
and in fact you lost the contributions of the allies
and ten talents.

It remains for me to tell you why it was that
Demosthenes wrote this decree, and how he got a
bribe of three talents for doing so,—one from Chalcis
through Callias, another from Eretria through their
king Clitarchus, and the remaining one from Oreum.
The bargain was found out in this way. Oreum was
a democracy, and all its public matters were trans-
acted through decrees. The people had been much
exhausted in their war with Philip, and left almost
without resources. They therefore sent Gnosidemus
son of Charigenes their old ruler to Demosthenes to
beg him to remit the payment of this talent, offering
at the same time to erect his statue in brass in their
city. Demosthenes replied to him that he had no
need of the smallest piece of brass, and that he would
procure payment of his talent through Callias. The
Oreans thus driven to close quarters, and being with-

out money, were obliged to hypothecate their public revenues to Demosthenes as a security for the talent, and paid him as interest upon the price of his venality at the rate of a drachma a month for a mina, until they had discharged the principal. And this was all done by a decree of the people. Take it and read it in proof of my statement.

DECREE.

This decree is at the same time dishonorable to our City, a strong proof of the character of Demosthenes's political acts, and a conclusive accusation of Ctesiphon. It is impossible that the recipient of such degrading bribes can be the exemplary citizen which this man has dared to call him in his decree.

I come now to the third period to which I have referred, a period the most disastrous of all, in which Demosthenes whelmed in a common ruin the affairs of our own State and of all Greece by his impiety towards the Delphian temple, and by the iniquitous and unfair alliance he brought about with Thebes. I shall begin with his sacrilegious acts to the Gods.

There is a plain, Athenians, called Kirrha, and a post now termed infamous and accursed. This country was formerly inhabited by the Kirrhæans and Acragallidæ, a people regardless of law, who profaned the temple of Delphi, plundered the sacred offerings to it, and even insulted the Amphictyons. Our ancestors in particular, as tradition reports, and

then the other Amphictyons, indignant at these outrages, consulted the oracle to learn from the divinity
in what way they should punish these guilty men.
The response was, to make incessant war upon them,
to ravage their country, and, after subduing and en-
slaving the inhabitants, to consecrate the ground to
the Pythian Apollo, to Artemis, to Latona, and to
Athene the Provident, and to leave it unworked forever, neither cultivating it themselves nor permitting
it to be done by others. When this response was
received, the Amphictyons, acting under the advice
of Solon that eminent law-giver distinguished alike
as a poet and philosopher, resolved to march against
those accursed men in fulfilment of the oracle of the
God; and having assembled a sufficient force, they
conquered and enslaved the inhabitants, filled up
their harbors, razed their cities to the ground, and
consecrated the territory in obedience to the oracle.
Furthermore they obliged themselves by oath never
to cultivate the soil, nor to permit others to do it, but
to defend the city and to preserve the ground unpro-
faned, with all their strength and might. Nor were
they content with simply swearing this oath, but they
further bound themselves by maledictions and imprecations upon themselves should they ever violate
it. For it was thus set forth in this terrible formula,
"that if any city, people, or private person, shall
transgress this oath, let them be held accursed of
Apollo, of Artemis, of Latona, and of Athene the

Provident! Let not the earth yield to them its fruits, nor let their wives bring forth children like unto their parents, but unseemly monsters; let not their flocks and herds give increase in the order of nature; let their people ever fail in war, and in their civil controversies and in trade; and may they be utterly destroyed, they, their households, and their children. And finally, may their offerings never be acceptable nor received by Artemis, Latona, or the wise Athene!"

In proof of this let the oracle be now read. Listen to the imprecations, and recall the oaths sworn by your ancestors in common with the Amphictyons.

ORACLE.

"The city's towers ne'er taken shall not fall,
   Till dark-eyed Amphitrite with her waves
   Shall bathe the sacred fields with hollow moan."

OATHS—IMPRECATIONS.

In spite of these imprecations, these oaths, this oracle, yet engraven in the sacred archives, the Locrians of Amphissa, or rather their chiefs, wickedest and most disloyal of men, entered upon the sacred plain, cultivated it, rebuilt and occupied the accursed port, exacted imposts from those who visited it, and corrupted with bribes many of the deputies who were sent to Delphi, Demosthenes among the rest. For having been elected a deputy by you, he received a thousand drachmas from the Amphissians to keep

silence in regard to them in the Council of the
Amphictyons. And it was further agreed that for
the future twenty minæ should be sent every year to
him at Athens out of their sacrilegious funds, upon
condition that he should assist them there with all
his strength. Whence it occurred, even more than
theretofore, that every one who was handled by him
—individual, prince or commonwealth—became involved in irremediable evils.

But consider here, men of Athens, how the Divinity and Fortune were superior to the impiety of
the Amphissians. In the archonship of Theophras-
tus and in the presbytership of Diognetus the Anaphlystian, you chose as deputies Midias of Anagyrus,
(who for many reasons I could wish were now living,)
Thrasycles of Olus, and myself. When we reached
Delphi it so chanced that Diognetus the presbyter
was taken ill of a fever, and Midias along with him.
The Amphictyons were then in session; and we were
informed by some of our well-wishers that the Amphissians, who were crouching under the rule of the
Thebans and altogether subservient to them, had introduced a decree against our City by which it was
proposed to mulct us in a fine of fifty talents for
having suspended in the new temple before its consecration, golden shields with this true inscription
upon them :—" taken by the Athenians from the
Persians and Thebans when they fought together
against the Greeks." I was requested by our pres-

byter to repair to the Assembly and to speak on behalf of the City before the Amphictyons, and I had proposed the same thing to myself. My fellow-deputies being absent, I entered the Assembly with some degree of warmth and began to speak. Immediately an insolent, and, as it seemed to me, an illiterate fellow from among the Amphissians, perhaps urged on by some unpropitious deity to commit the outrage, cried out, "Men of Greece, if you are wise, let not even the name of the Athenian people be uttered here at this time, but drive them from the temple as execrable." And he forthwith recalled our alliance with the Phocians which had been proposed by Crobylus, and ran over many other indecent charges against the City, which I had neither patience to listen to then, nor have satisfaction in recounting now.

I heard him with a spirit of indignation such as I had never before felt, and rose to reply. What I said in answer to him I shall pass over, with a single exception. But in concluding it came into my head to speak of the impiety of the Amphissians in regard to the sacred territory. From the place where I stood I pointed to the Kirrhæan plain;—it lies, you know, almost under the temple, and can be readily seen from it.—"Look," I exclaimed, "Amphictyons, look upon this plain now cultivated by the Amphissians, behold their factories and their workshops built all over it. You see with your own eyes that infamous and ac-

cursed harbor entirely reconstructed. You know of
your own knowledge, and need no other witnesses,
that they have levied imposts for its use, and are now
receiving money from this sacred port." And at the
same time I ordered to be read to them the oracle of
the God, the oath of their ancestors, and the imprecations pronounced by them; and I affirmed that on
behalf of the people of Athens, myself, my children,
and my household, I would according to the oath
assist the God, and the consecrated ground, by hand
and foot and voice, and with my whole strength, until
I had acquitted my country of her duty to the Gods.
"Do you," I thus proceeded, "see to it as to yourselves. The sacred panniers are now being elevated,
the victims are at the foot of the altar, and you are
about to ask of the Gods blessings for yourselves,
and for your common country. With what voice,
with what spirit, with what eyes, with what assurance,
shall you address to them your prayers, while you
still leave these wicked wretches unpunished who are
involved in this anathema? The imprecation is express, not written in enigmas, but in words of light
both as to the punishment which awaits these impious
men, and you yourselves who are passively upholding
them in their crimes. This is its language: 'Those
who abstain from punishing these men, can neither
make acceptable sacrifice to Apollo, to Artemis, to
Latona, or to Athene the Provident, nor shall their
offerings be received.'"

After I had thus spoken and much more to the same purpose, I quitted the Assembly and went out. Immediately a great cry arose and the excitement was great among the Amphictyons. Their talk was no longer about the shields which had been hung up by us, but about punishing the Amphissians. The day was already far spent, and the herald came forward and proclaimed that the men of Delphi who were of the age of twenty and upwards, whether free or bond, should assemble on the morrow at the break of day, with scythes and spades, at a place called Tytheum. And the same herald announced that the presbyters and deputies should meet in the same place in order to give assistance to the God and the sacred plain; and any city which absented itself should be excluded from the temple, held accursed, and involved in the imprecation.

The next day at dawn we came together at the appointed spot, and descending to the Kirrhæan plain, destroyed the port and burnt the houses, and were about to retire. But whilst we were thus engaged, the Locrians of Amphissa, who dwelt at the distance of about sixty stadia from Delphi, came against us with their whole people in arms, and we were in danger of being cut off had we not escaped with difficulty by flight to Delphi.

On the day following, Cottyphus, who was charged with the duty of collecting the votes, convoked a General Assembly of the Amphictyons. It was styled

a General Assembly when it consisted not only of
the deputies and presbyters, but of those who came
thither to sacrifice to and consult the God. At its
convocation numerous accusations were preferred
against the Amphissians, and great praise was given
to our City. As a result of their deliberations, it was
decreed that the presbyters should come to Thermopylæ at a designated day, in advance of the next
Assembly, armed with a decree by virtue of which
the Amphissians should be punished for the acts of
impiety they had committed against the God, the
sacred territory and the Amphictyons. The clerk
will now read this decree to corroborate my statements.

DECREE.

This decree having been presented by us upon our
return to the Senate, and again to the people in the
Assembly, our action was ratified and the whole City
was on the side of the God. Demosthenes nevertheless by reason of the pay he had received from
the Amphissians resolved to oppose it, but I overcame him plainly in your presence. Finding that he
could not deceive the City, as the evidence was too
plain, he came into the Senate, and having caused all
private citizens to retire he brought into the Assembly a preliminary decree which he had had passed
through the inexperience of the mover. He succeeded in obtaining the passage of this decree by
the people in the Assembly, although it had already

risen, and most of the members had left, I myself among the rest, or I would never have permitted it. Its summary is as follows: " The Athenian presbyter and the present and future deputies shall report themselves at Thermopylæ and Delphi at the time designated by our ancestors."—Fair enough in form, but scandalous in fact, this decree prevented our joining the convocation which was necessarily to be convened at Thermopylæ before the regular Assembly should meet.—And moreover he had inserted in the same decree another article still plainer and more pointed, as follows:—" The Athenian presbyter and deputies present and future shall in no wise participate either in the deliberations, conduct, or decrees of the deputies in any way whatsoever."—In no wise participate?—Shall I speak truth as to this clause, or shall I only utter what is pleasant to listen to?—I shall speak out the truth! It is these honey-tongued utterances which have brought the City to her present condition!—This language meant that we were to be permitted to remember neither the oaths sworn by our ancestors, the imprecations pronounced by them, nor the oracle of the God.

In consequence of this decree, men of Athens, we remained at home, while the other Amphictyons reassembled at Thermopylæ with the exception of a single city whose name I cannot mention;—may her misfortunes be kept far away from the other Greeks! And it was resolved at this meeting that an expedition should be undertaken against the Amphissians, and the same Cottyphus the Pharsalian who had collected the votes of the Assembly was chosen general. Philip, whom Demosthenes will soon dare to assert I brought down against the Greeks, was not then in Macedonia, nor even in Greece, but absent far away in Scythia. In this first expedition great moderation was shewn towards the Amphissians, for they were simply punished for their great misdeeds by a fine which was directed to be paid to the God by a certain day; the accursed authors of the outrages were banished, and those who had quitted the country in consequence of the sacrilege were restored to it. When indeed the Amphissians refused to discharge the fine, brought back the criminals, and expelled the pious citizens who had been recalled, a second armament was organized against them. But this was a long time afterwards, upon Philip's return from his expedition against the Scythians, when the venality of Demosthenes had proved the obstacle to our obtaining the command of the sacred war which the immortal Gods had committed to us.

Did not, Athenians, did not the Gods forewarn us, did they not declare to us almost with the significance of a human utterance, to be upon our guard against the impending danger? Never have I known a State more completely under the protection of the Gods, never have I seen one more completely ruined by certain of its public men! The prodigies which accompanied the mysteries, the death of the newly initiated, should not all this have been sufficient to excite our apprehensions? Did not Aminiades warn us of our danger, and beg us to send persons to Delphi to interrogate the divinity and ascertain from him what was to be done? Was not all this opposed by Demosthenes, who, brutally misusing the license you had accorded to him, even declared that the oracle was philippizing? And when the consummation was at hand and the sacrifices were unpropitious and unacceptable to the Gods, did he .not send out our soldiers to certain peril? Yes, this very man who recently dared to assert that Philip had not entered our territory because the sacrifices were unfavorable to him!—What punishment do you not merit, scourge of all Greece?—If the conqueror was deterred from marching into the conquered country because the auguries forbade it, and if in absolute ignorance of futurity without one happy omen you sent forward our soldiers to a certain doom, do you deserve to be now honored with a crown for the ruin you have brought upon the State, or to be forever banished from it?

Truly, Athenians, what unexpected, what unforeseen events have occurred in our day! We have not lived the ordinary life of mortals, but we have been born to be the wonder of posterity. The Persian King, the mighty monarch who cut through Mount Athos, who chained the Hellespont, who demanded

of the Greeks earth and water, who dared to write
that he was master of all nations from the rising to
the setting sun, is he not now contending not for the
mastery of others, but for his own personal existence?
And have we not seen the very men who delivered
the temple of Delphi judged worthy of the glory of
the command against the Persian? And Thebes our
neighboring city, has not Thebes been swept in a
single day from the face of Greece? And if not
unjustly, because they managed their affairs impru-
dently and stupidly, still they seem rather to have
been struck with judicial blindness, than to have
shewn mere human ignorance and folly. And the
unhappy Lacedemonians who interfered but slightly
in the beginning in the attack upon the temple, the
people who formerly aspired to be the leaders of
Greece, are now compelled to send hostages to Alexander, and to display their misery before the whole
world, reduced to suffer for themselves and country
what the pleasure of the conqueror may inflict, and to
expect that moderation which an enemy who has received the first offence may choose to shew them.
And our own City, heretofore the common refuge
of all Greeks, to whom in former days embassies
from every State in Greece were wont to come to
claim our protection, no longer now contends for
empire, but for her own soil.

And this has all been brought to pass since Demosthenes began to intervene in public affairs. Well

does the poet Hesiod express himself upon this subject, when he seeks to instruct the people, and to counsel republics to shut their ears to the advances of designing demagogues. I will repeat his verses: for doubtless we were taught in childhood to commit to memory these noble sentences of the poets, that we might store them up for use in our mature age:

> "Oft do whole nations pay the guilt of one
> Who by his crimes insults an angry heaven!
> Famine and plague, twin ministers of wrath,
> Great Saturn's son sends forth: armies perish,
> Towers and strongholds fall, and mighty fleets
> Are swept away, in witness of Jove's ire."

Take away Hesiod's metre, and consider only the thoughts to which he gave expression, and you shall no longer regard it as the language of poetry, but as an oracle pointed at the administration of Demosthenes:—an army, a naval expedition, many cities, have been in fact all annihilated through this man's policy.

I think indeed that neither Phrynondas, nor Eurybatus, nor any other of the traitors of old, was ever such a charlatan and impostor as this fellow. He dares indeed, (I call heaven and earth to witness, and ye divinities and all men who wish to hear the truth!) he dares to look you in the face, and to assert that the Thebans entered into the alliance with you, not driven to it by the force of circumstances, by stress of the

fear in which they found themselves, not by reason
of your own glory, but in consequence of the harangues of Demosthenes! And yet before his time,
those who were best inclined to the Thebans went
many times as ambassadors to Thebes without success; first of all Thrasybulus of Collytta, a man honored with their entire confidence,—then Thraso their
patron in our City, Leodamas the Acharnian whose
eloquence was not inferior to that of Demosthenes
and to me at least a much more pleasing speaker,
Archidemus another eloquent man whose regard for
the Thebans had exposed him to many dangers during his administration, Aristophon the Azenian who
labored for a long time under the imputation of The-
banizing, and lastly Pyrandrus of Anaphlystus who
is still alive. No one was ever able to secure their
friendship for you. The reason I know well, but I
care not now to mention it, out of regard to the Thebans' misfortunes. But after Philip had taken Nicæa
from them and handed it over to the Thessalians,
after he had in traversing Phocis again brought upon
them the war which he had before kept away from
Bœotia, and finally after he had taken and fortified
Elatea and planted a garrison in it, then when present danger menaced them, then it was that the Thebans had recourse to you, and you marched out to
their relief and entered Thebes with your troops both
horse and foot, before Demosthenes had written a
single syllable about the alliance. The times, their

alarm, and the need of union with you, brought you to Thebes, not Demosthenes.

In this matter of the treaty, moreover, Demosthenes committed three capital faults to your prejudice.   First, when Philip who was at war merely in name with Athens, but had his whole hostility really directed against the Thebans as events proved, (and why say more on this point?) Demosthenes kept this important consideration entirely out of view; and pretending that the alliance had been brought about not from the stress of circumstances but through his own embassies, he persuaded you that it was of less consequence to discuss the conditions of the alliance than to succeed in obtaining it.   Having secured this point, he abandoned all Bœotia to the Thebans by the introduction of a clause into the treaty that if any city should revolt from Thebes the Athenians should be bound to assist only the Bœotians who adhered to Thebes.   He thus concealed and evaded the real issue, according to his wont, by delusive language; as if the Bœotians when smarting under injury would content themselves with Demosthenes's fine phrases, and not rather feel indignant at the real injustice they were made to suffer. Again, he assessed you from whom the danger was remote with two-thirds of the expense of the war, charging the Thebans with the other third; being well paid for this and his other arrangements.   The command of the fleet he divided, while he put the

whole cost upon you; but he gave up, to speak
plainly, the entire control of the land forces to the
Thebans, insomuch that Stratocles your general was
unable during the war to provide even for the safety
of his own troops.   I accuse him not as to matters
which others might pass over, but I speak out as to
what all condemn him for; and yet you who know
all this express no resentment about it.   You seem
to be disposed towards Demosthenes in this way:
you have been so accustomed to hear of his misdeeds, that they no longer create astonishment in
you.   But you must put away this frame of mind,
and become indignant unto punishment, if you are
to expect that even what is left to our State shall
prosper.

But there was a second wrong committed by him
even greater than the first.   By means of the clause
which provided for the common consideration of all
measures with the chiefs of Bœotia he practically
abstracted from our Senate and people the entire
discussion of public business, and transported it to
Thebes, to the Cadmeia. 'In this way his power
became so absolute, that he publicly announced to
you from the platform, that he would go as ambassador whithersoever he thought proper, without regard
to your orders.

Did any of your generals differ from him in
opinion, he declared he would reduce them to submission and accustom them to absolute acquiescence

by having the pre-eminence of the platform established over that of the camp, asserting that you had been more benefited by his efforts from the platform than by anything done by any general in the field. Besides making profit out of the empty battalions in our foreign forces and embezzling the soldiers' pay, he hired out to the Amphissians ten thousand of these troops against my reiterated protests and objectious in the Assembly; and in consequence of their removal he involved the City in serious peril.\ What, think you, could Philip have most desired under the circumstances? Was it not to fight here separately against the City's forces, separately in Amphissa against the mercenaries, and then after striking such a blow to surprise the discouraged Greeks? And the author of all this ruin, not content with escaping the punishment due to his offences, is indignant, forsooth, at being deprived of the honor of a golden crown! And it is not enough for him that it shall be proclaimed in presence of you his fellow-citizens, but he must complain bitterly if it be not done before the eyes of assembled Greece! Thus, it seems, a depraved nature armed with great power brings heavy calamities upon the State.

The third and by much the most important offence which I have referred to, I am now about to speak of. Philip did not despise the Greeks. He was quite too intelligent for that. Nor was he so inconsiderate as to desire to risk upon the event of the

fraction of a day all the advantages he had secured.
He was therefore desirous of an accommodation, and
was upon the point of sending envoys to treat about
it. The Theban magistrates also rightly apprehended
the impending danger; for they had learned a lesson
not easily to be forgotten from the Phocian war of
ten years' duration :—they needed not the advice of
an unwarlike orator, who had been guilty of desert-
ing his post. In this condition of things, Demosthenes suspecting that the Bœotian leaders had been
secretly bribed by Philip to conclude a particular
peace, and thinking it worse than death that he
should be left out of the circle of corruption, burst
into the Assembly when there was no question under
consideration of either peace or war; and intending
to proclaim in advance as if through the voice of a
herald to the Theban magistrates that they must give
him a share of the plunder, he swore by Athene
(whose statue Phidias seems to have carved to enable
Demosthenes to appeal to as an instrument of perjury
and profit) that if any one should speak of making
peace with Philip he would drag him to prison by
the hair of his head, in imitation of that Cleophon
who, we are told, ruined the republic by his violence
in the war with the Lacedemonians. But as the
Thebans paid no heed to him, and were even about
sending back your troops who had already taken
the field, maddened at the spectacle, he ascended
the platform and denounced the Bœotian rulers as

traitors to Greece. And the man who had never dared to look the foe in the face, declared that he would introduce a decree under which you would send deputies to the Thebans to demand a passage through their country against Philip! Those who were in power there, mortified and dreading that they might really appear to have betrayed the cause of the Greeks, faltered and turned aside from all thoughts of peace, and threw themselves into preparations for the conflict.

It is here the proper place to speak of the gallant men whom this Demosthenes in disregard of unpropitious auspices sent forth to meet a certain doom. The wretch who mounts the tombs of these unhappy victims with the trembling feet which faltered in the ranks and fled from battle, is he who dares to celebrate the courage of these heroes! Oh most dastardly of men, most incapable of wise and noble conduct, but most audaciously skilful in the use of words, darest thou now to undertake to look upon the countenances of these thy fellow-citizens, and to assert before them that thou deservest to be crowned for bringing ruin upon thy country! And if he dares to say this, will you my fellow-citizens permit it, and shall the memory of those brave men perish with them, when they have ceased to live? Go with me for a moment in your thoughts from this tribunal to the theatre, behold the herald advancing slowly, and listen to the proclamation which will follow this decree. Will the parents and the relatives of these unfortunate soldiers shed more abundant tears over the misfortunes and woes presented in the tragic spectacles there exhibited, than over the State's ingratitude? What Greek trained in the principles of freedom will not on such a day be filled with grief when he reflects that formerly before the spectacles began, when the government was administered under happier laws and by wiser counsellors, the herald would advance with the youthful orphans whose fathers had fallen in the field, and pointing to them clad in complete armor would proclaim in those beautiful and encouraging words, "Behold the children of the gallant men who lost their lives in our defence, whom their country has educated up to manhood, and now presents here armed in proof, and sends forth with happy auguries to manage their own affairs and to aspire to the highest honors of the State."

Such was the language of the herald in former days, but now how different! Were he now to present before you him who caused the orphanhood of all these children, in what terms think you would he make his proclamation? Should he indeed recite the form of the decree, truth would cry out and proclaim our shame in words of contradiction to the herald's voice. She would assert that the Athenian people crown for his virtue the man, if he be a man, who is infamous for vice,—for his courage, the

coward who in the hour of danger fled from his post !
I implore you, men of Athens, in the name of the
sovereign Jove and all the Gods, suffer not to be
erected against yourselves a trophy in the temple of
Dionysus; convict not our City of madness in the
face of assembled Greece; nor remind the world of
the irremediable woes of the unhappy Thebans whom
you welcomed hither when they fled from the homes
from which they had been driven by the venality of
Demosthenes, through whose corruption they lost
their temples, their children, and their tombs.

But since you were not present in person, figure
to yourselves in imagination the condition of this
unhappy people. Their city is carried by assault;
amidst the horrors and confusion of walls overturned, and houses in flames, you shall see women
and children driven from their homes into slavery,
and aged persons of both sexes unlearning too late
in life the sweet teachings of freedom; you shall
find them in all their misery less indignant against
the immediate instruments of their punishment than
against the real authors of their wrongs: they implore you with sobs and tears never to honor with a
crown the scourge of Greece, but to guard yourselves
against the evil genius and the ill-fortune which have
always accompanied this man. No community, no
private person has ever prospered who has submitted
himself to the counsels of Demosthenes. And will
you not be ashamed, Athenians, after enacting a law

about the passage over the Strait to Salamis, that
any ferryman who shall even unintentionally upset
his boat shall never again be permitted to exercise
his calling, that no one through carelessness may
jeopard the lives of Greeks, yet to allow this man,
who has so completely destroyed not only Athens
but all Greece, to be placed again at the head of our
government?

In coming now to the fourth period, which em-
braces our present condition, I wish first to remind
you that Demosthenes not only quitted the ranks of
the army on the battle-field, but also deserted his
post as a citizen; for he embarked on one of your
vessels, and immediately started off under pretext of
levying contributions upon the other Greeks. When
the danger had unexpectedly passed away, he returned to Athens, and advancing towards the platform trembling and half dead with fear, he besought
you to elect him commissioner for settling the terms
of peace. At that time you would not even suffer
the name of Demosthenes to be inscribed upon your
decrees, but injoined the duty upon Nausicles : and
yet he now demands the honor of a crown ! After
Philip's assassination, and Alexander had succeeded
to the throne, he resumed his trade of impostor. He
erected altars to Pausanias, drew upon the Senate the
odium of ordering sacrifices at the good news, and
even termed the new king a Margites, assuring us he
would never stir from Macedon, but remain at Pella

walking about watching the auguries. All this, he
said, he asserted positively and not from conjecture,
since courage is purchased by blood alone. This
fellow thus spoke, who was without blood in his own
veins, and who judged Alexander not after Alexander's nature, but from his own dastardly character!
But when the Thessalians were marching against
your City, and the youthful monarch was animated
with a just anger, his army actually investing Thebes,
Demosthenes, who had been chosen ambassador to
him, took the alarm on Mount Cithæron, and returned flying back to Athens, thus proving himself
equally useless in peace and in war. And most
astonishing· of all, you have not surrendered this
man for trial by the Assembly of the Greeks;—the
traitor who, if common report is true, has betrayed
you all!

According to the statements of the mariners and
of your envoys to Alexander,—and the thing seems
highly probable,—there went with them a young
man from Platæa, Aristion the son of Aristobulus
the druggist, whom some of you are perhaps acquainted with. This youth, who was of remarkable
personal beauty, lived for a long time in the house of
Demosthenes, upon what footing is uncertain, and it
would be improper for me to explain. Taking advantage, as I have heard, of the belief that his origin
and former mode of life were unknown, he insinuated
himself into Alexander's favor, and was admitted

into his intimacy.   Through this man Demosthenes
corresponded with the king, and by flattery and ob-
sequiousness secured a certain foothold for reconcilia-
tion.   And observe how the facts agree with what I
allege against him.

If Demosthenes really believed what he now asserts,
and was so hostile, as he says he was, to Alexander,
three fine opportunities for proving this presented
themselves, none of which he made use of.

First of all, when Alexander, just seated on the
throne, was about passing over into Asia, his
authority at home not yet firmly established, the
Persian king, then in his prime of strength, abound-
ing in ships, and troops and supplies of all kinds,
would readily have made an alliance with us on account of the dangers which threatened him.   What
word did you then utter, Demosthenes, or what decree did you prepare?   Shall I set down this omis-
sion to your fears, and to your native timidity?   Yet
public policy waits not upon the cowardice of the
public man.

Again, when Darius had descended with all his
powers, and Alexander was menaced in Cilicia,
without support, and as you then said, about to be
crushed by the Persian cavalry; when Athens could
scarce contain your insolence, and you strutted about
the streets with letters in your hands, pointing out
my face as that of a terror-stricken man, and saying
I was a victim crowned for the sacrifice ready to fall

at the least reverse to Alexander;—even then you did nothing, but waited for a more favorable opportunity. But passing over all this, I will come down to the present moment.

The Lacedemonians, with the aid of a foreign force, had gained a battle, defeating a Macedonian army near Corragus: the Elians had joined them, all the Achæans except the people of Pellene, all Arcadia, except Megalopolis. That city was besieged, and every day was expected to be taken. Alexander himself had advanced beyond the Great Bear, and almost beyond the habitable globe: Antipater had for a long time been trying to gather together an army, and the future was uncertain. Tell us now, Demosthenes, what you then did, what you then said; if you will, I yield to you the platform until you shall have finished. You are silent and embarrassed; I take compassion upon you, and will now report myself what you then rehearsed.

Do you not remember, Athenians, the odious and almost incredible language which he then uttered, and which you then listened to with the callousness of steel, when, advancing from the platform, he cried out, " There are some among you who clip and cut the City as a vine, who hack the people's tendrils; the very nerves of the State have been cut asunder, we are stitched up as in a mat, our sides are pricked as with needles." What language was this, oh beast, was it words, or the utterance of a monster! And

again, when swinging yourself round upon the platform you gave yourself out as working against Alexander, and bawled out, " It is I who raised up against
him the Lacedemonians, it is I who detached from
him the Thessalians and Perrhibœans."—You, Demosthenes, you stir up a single burgh! You, who
would never come near a town, or even a single
house, where danger was present! But if money
was anywhere to be spent, there you were sure to be
found;—never whère a deed of manhood was to be
done! Is a lucky stroke struck, you cunningly ap-
propriate it, and take care to inscribe it with your
name; is danger in the wind, you ever keep out of
the way; but with the return of confidence, you cry
out for recompense, for rewards and golden crowns!

Oh, but he is a friend of the people, a lover of our
institutions! If you turn to his flattering harangues,
you will be deceived as you have ever been: if you
scan his real nature, and look at the truth itself, you
will be saved from error. And thus should you
make up your judgment about him. But I will now
consider with you the true character of the wise and
virtuous friend of his country, contrasting with it the
vile partisan of the government of a few; and when
you have both presented for comparison, then search
out and prove which of the two he is, not from his
own fawning tongue, but from his life and conduct.

You will all doubtless admit that the true patriot
should first of all be liberally born both on the father's

and the mother's side, lest he might look with disfavor, by reason of his misfortune, upon our free democratic constitution. Next, he should be able to point
to services rendered by his ancestors to the State; or
at least that they should not have laid themselves
open to reproach, lest in the effort to remedy their
disgrace he might be brought to do the Commonwealth a wrong. Thirdly, his daily walk in life
should be wise and moderate, that waste and irregu-
larity may not tempt him to take the wages of corruption to the people's disadvantage. Fourthly, he
should be able to clothe noble and patriotic thoughts
in fitting language, that he may the better appeal
to right intelligence; for the persuasive wisdom of
the speaker powerfully influences his auditors. But
good sense must always be set above mere rhetorical display. Lastly, he must be of firm and con-
stant heart, that he may never be tempted to abandon
his fellow-citizens in the face of danger. He who
adheres to the power of an oligarchy is the opposite
of all this, and it is useless to repeat his characteristics. Examine then well, which of the patriot's
attributes belong to Demosthenes; but let the examination be in all respects fair and just.

His father, Demosthenes of Pæania, was undoubtedly a man of free birth; this must be fully admitted.
But how about his descent on the mother's side, and
who was his maternal grandfather? I will tell you.
There was once a certain Gylon of Kerameis who

betrayed to the enemy Nymphæum, a city of Pontus
which then belonged to us; and being denounced for
this, he awaited not the sentence of death, but fled
from Athens and settled on the Bosphorus. He received from the neighboring princes as the reward of
his perfidy a place called Kepi, and married a woman
rich indeed and who brought him a large estate, but
a Scythian by birth. From this union sprang two
daughters, whom he sent hither with considerable
fortunes. One he established in marriage with a
citizen whom I do not mention, as I desire not to
make unnecessary enemies; the other was betrothed
to Demosthenes of Pæania, who disregarded the laws
of his country in espousing her. The issue of this
marriage was Demosthenes, this officious meddling
sycophant. On his mother's side, on her father's, he
is thus the people's enemy; for against his grandfather you pronounced sentence of death. His
mother, Greek only in speech, but barbarian by
race, has given the world a son whose wicked nature
proves him no true Athenian.

And what has been his daily mode of life? Having
wasted his inheritance by folly and frivolity, from a
trierarch he became a special pleader; but showing
his treachery in this employment by the betrayal of
his clients' secrets to their adversaries, he quitted it
to betake himself to the platform. Of the large sums
which he received from the public he kept little;
but the king of Persia's gold flowed freely to sup-

port his profusion. Yet all this proved insufficient, 'for no. money could satisfy the prodigality of his spendthrift nature. He lived, in a word, not from his private revenues, but from the public dangers.

But what are his endowments of ability and power of speech? Eloquent in words, his life is utterly depraved. Of his abuse of his body, and his coarse sensuality, I must not speak at large. To reveal the gross vices of our fellows is always an ungrateful task. But what does the City get by this?—Fine words, and ill deeds.

It remains to speak a word or two about his courage. Had he denied his cowardice, or were you not all well acquainted with it, I had had here the occasion of consuming a little time upon this point. But as he has avowed it himself in our Assemblies, and you are thoroughly informed about it, I need only refer to the laws which have been framed upon this subject. Our ancient law-giver Solon thought that the man who refused to obey the summons to the field, as well as he who quitted the ranks, were equally guilty with the coward: for the laws are enacted against cowardice. Should some of you perchance be surprised that a natural infirmity is treated as a crime, the reason is easily given. It is that each citizen fearing more the punishment inflicted by the laws than the enemy's face should contend all the better in his country's behalf. The law therefore excludes equally from the public lustrations the

man who refuses to serve, the coward, and him who
abandons his post.   He can neither receive the honor
of a crown, nor be admitted to the sacred rites of the
temple.   And yet you, Ctesiphon, order us to crown
a man incapable by law of receiving a crown; by
your decree you call into the theatre, during the
tragedies, him who is unworthy of appearing there;
you attempt to introduce into the temple of Dionysus
one who has forfeited through his cowardice all right
to participate in the rites of religion.

But, lest I should withdraw your attention from
the subject, keep this point steadily in view.   When
he professes his great affection for the people, look
to his life, not his words; regard what he is, not
what he says.   And as we are talking of crowns and
rewards, let me, while it is still in my mind, forewarn you, Athenians, that unless this prodigality of
honors, this indiscriminate conferring of crowns is
stopped, you will neither obtain the thanks of those
who are honored, nor will the affairs of the City be
advanced.   The worthless man will not be made
better, while the good will be altogether discouraged
by it.   Let me give you some pregnant instances of
the truth of what I say.   Were the question put to
you whether the condition of the State was more
glorious in your ancestors' time than at present, all
would answer, In the days of our forefathers.   Were
the men of the olden time better than now?   Then,
they were truly great; now, alas, how degenerate!

And crowns, and honors, and proclamations and entertainments in the Prytaneum, were they more rife then than now? In those days rewards with us were rare, but the name of virtue was truly precious. In our time honors have become vile by their profusion: and crowns are given as a customary ceremonial, not as a recompense conferred with judgment.

Should it seem strange to the reflecting mind that while honors *now* are more abundant, *then* the public interests more flourished, that public servants should *now* be worse, *then* better, I will endeavor to give the explanation. Can you suppose, Athenians, that any one would enter the lists of the Olympian Games, or of any other of our public sports to strive for the prize in wrestling or any other contest, were the crown awarded, not to the best man, but to some intriguing trickster? No! None would prepare himself for the encounter. It is because the prize is rare, hard to obtain, conferring immortality upon the victor, and therefore glorious, that the generous youth keep their bodies under subjection, endure the greatest hardships, and are ready to meet the greatest dangers! And imagine yourselves to be the judges in the contention for civic excellence; think you not that when you bestow the prize uprightly upon the deserving few, the combatants in this glorious strife will not be many? It is by showing favor to the ready caballer, that you stifle all noble aspirations.

Let me make my meaning still more plain. Which
was the better. man, Themistocles the commander of
your fleet when you overcame the Persians at Salamis, or Demosthenes the deserter from the ranks?—
Miltiades the conqueror at Marathon, or this fellow?
—the men who brought back from Phyle the flying
people, Aristides surnamed the just, or Demosthenes
who should be surnamed something very different?
But, by the Olympian Gods, it were unworthy to mention on the same day this beast and those illustrious
men! Let him show, if he can, when he comes to
speak, when was it it was ever decreed that a crown
should be conferred upon any of them. Was their
country then ungrateful? No! she was magnani-
mous: and these citizens were truly worthy of her,
in the very absence of such honors. They thought
it not honorable to be inscribed in decrees, but to
live in the remembrance of their grateful fellow-
citizens, which has kept their memory ever fresh
from that day down to this.

What then were their rewards? Such, indeed, as
it is honorable to speak of. There were those, Athenians, who, fighting under the greatest difficulties
and encountering the greatest perils, vanquished the
Persians near the river Strymon. On their arrival
here, the people accorded to their demand for recompense, what then seemed a mighty honor. In the
portico of the temple of Hermes were erected three
statues of the God, inscribed not with their own

names, lest the inscription should appear to be made for the generals, rather than the people. The language proves the truth of my assertion; for on the first you find these words:

> "Honor to those who first by Strymon's floods
> Routed the Mede, hard by old Eion's towers:
> Famine and valor laid the foeman low."

Upon the second:

> "Good-will and courage Athens thus rewards
> In those who forth her armies led. Let all,
> Of this regardful, strive to emulate
> This virtue in the State's behalf displayed."

And on the third Hermes it is thus inscribed:

> "In days of yore Menestheus to Troy's plains
> With great Atrides marched the Attic hosts:
> A mighty chieftain with the mail-clad Greeks
> The blind bard sings him. Hence the City claims
> Of War and Peace to stand the Arbiter."

Where do you find here the names of the generals? —Nowhere.—It is the people's only. Go with me, in imagination, to the painted Portico, for in this public place the monuments of all your glories are displayed in full view. Why do I ask this? It is because you will there find represented by the painter's hand the battle of Marathon. Should it be asked who led the troops to action on that glorious day, all would reply, Miltiades. Is his name inscribed there? Or did he ask this honor? The

State refused his claim, and only conceded that he should be there depicted leading on his troops to victory. Behold again in the temple of the Mother of the Gods, near the Senate-house, the record of the rewards bestowed upon the men who brought back our fugitive citizens from Phyle. The decree was proposed and passed by Archines of Koile, himself one of the victorious leaders, and by it was given to them, first, a largess of one thousand drachmas for sacrifices and offerings,—less than ten drachmas to each man. Next, they are all directed to be crowned with olive wreaths, not crowns of gold. The olive crown was precious in those days, while now the golden one is fallen into contempt. Nor was this honor distributed by chance. No, it was awarded after exact inquiry by the Senate to the men who had courageously sustained the siege in Phyle against the Lacedemonians and the Thirty, not to those who refused to keep their ranks at Chæronea against the enemy's attack. Listen to the decree in proof of my statements.

DECREE RELATING TO THE HONOR OF THOSE WHO HAD BEEN AT PHYLE.

Read now Ctesiphon's decree in favor of the author of all our ills.

DECREE.

The honor to the men of Phyle is effaced by this decree. If this last is right, the first one was all wrong.   If Thrasybulus and his companions were justly honored, Demosthenes is unjustly crowned.

He will assert however, I am told, that I act unfairly in comparing him with the men of the olden time, and will say that Philammon was not crowned at the Olympian Games for having overcome Glaucus that ancient wrestler, but for having defeated the combatants of the present day.   Fool! do we not know that athletes strive each with the other, but that in the struggle for the honors of the State the contest is with Virtue herself!   The herald's voice, when he proclaims the crown before assembled Greece, should echo back the truth!   Show us not, then, Demosthenes, that you have surpassed the pigmy Pataekion, but when you reclaim the honors of the State prove your title by your own worth. Let the clerk now read the inscription to the honor of the men who brought back the people from Phyle, lest I should seem to wander from the point.

INSCRIPTION.

" Athens, this soil which holds by ancient right,
   Honors with crowns of olive the brave men
   Who lightly prizing life the State redeemed
   By tyrants and by tyrants' laws oppressed."

The poet tells us these heroes were honored because they overthrew the men who governed contrary to law; for it was ringing in the ears of all that the people were defeated the moment there was taken from them the power to pursue the invaders of the law.

I have heard from my father, who lived to the age of ninety after sharing in all the misfortunes of his country, whilst conversing with me in his leisure moments, that upon the return of the people both words and deeds were equally punished when a prosecution was instituted for a violation of the laws. What more impious indeed than an assault against them either by speech or act? And according to his report, the trial was conducted not as at present, but the dicasts themselves were much more severe against the offenders than the prosecutor. Oftentimes would they call upon the clerk to read over the laws and 'the decree, and those accused of introducing bills in contravention of them were condemned not for transgressing the whole body of the laws, but for changing in them a single syllable. As the matter is now managed, the whole thing is ridiculous. The proposed illegal decree is read, while the jurors, inattentive to what is going on, listen as to a ballad or an idle tale. And you have furthermore, in following this fellow's artifices, introduced into our trials a scandalous practice. The rights of the State are completely reversed: it is the prosecutor who must defend himself, while the criminal attacks; and the judges, perplexed and in ignorance of the real point to be decided, are compelled to render their verdict upon something which is not before them. If the accused should perchance speak to the case at all, he defends himself not upon the ground of legality, but because another who has committed the self-same act has been heretofore suffered to escape scot-free. And upon this, I understand, Ctesiphon relies with great confidence.

Aristophon the Azenian once boasted in public that although he had been seventy-five times prosecuted for infractions of the law, he had never been convicted. How different was that ancient minister, the patriot Kephalus! His boast was—and it was an honest one—that while he had written more decrees than any, he had never been accused of violating the law. For in those days, not only did political opponents accuse each other of illegality, but friends withstood friends upon the ground of injustice done the State. Here is a striking proof. When Archines accused Thrasybulus of illegality for proposing a crown to one of those who had returned with him from Phyle, the prosecution was successful in spite of the recent great services of the accused. For the jurors thought that the same Thrasybulus who had brought back our countrymen from Phyle to the City, himself drove them forth again, in thus proposing an illegal decree. To-day all is different. Your generals of repute, your public men honored by maintenance in the Prytaneum, solicit you on behalf of the violators of the law. And you should rightly treat them as ungrateful citizens. For the

man who, honored by a democracy like ours which
is protected by Heaven and the laws, dares to assist
the laws' infringer, himself attempts the destruction
of the very State from which he draws his title to
consideration.

What then should be the course a just and wise
man should adopt in such a defence as this? I will
expose it. When an impeachment founded upon the
proposal of an illegal decree is brought before the
Court, one-third of the day of trial should be accorded to the accuser, to the laws and to the government. The second part should then be given to
the accused and his defenders. If the defence is not
successful upon the first vote, the remaining portion
of the day should be consumed in adjusting the sentence in proportion to the crime. To solicit your
moderation in awarding it, is nothing but an appeal
to your clemency: but to ask your suffrages in the
first instance in behalf of the offender, is to ask you
to run counter to your oaths, the laws, and the constitution. It is to ask what is equally unlawful either
for them to solicit or for you to grant. You should
then compel these importunate petitioners to suffer
you first to pronounce your verdict in conformity
to law, and then ask you to abate the rigor of the
sentence.

For my own part, Athenians, I am strongly inclined to the opinion that in prosecutions for an infraction of the law like this, it should be forbidden

both to the accuser and the accused to employ an advocate. In such cases the law of justice is plain and
easily determined. For as in the construction of a
building a supposed departure from the perpendic-
ular is settled by the plumb-line, so in an accusation
for a breach of law by means of the proposal of an
illegal decree, a plain and simple rule is placed before the judge in the record upon which the laws and
the decree attacked are inscribed. Shew that the
decree conforms to the law, and then, Ctesiphon, descend. Why must you call upon Demosthenes? To
pass by a just defence, and then to claim the services
of an architect of evil, a weaver of harangues, in this
way you arrest the cause of justice, you injure the
City, and you defeat the constitution.

How must we get rid of all such artifice? Should
Ctesiphon step forward and rehearse the introduction of that discourse which has been prepared for
him, and then proceed to waste your time in empty
declamation without touching his defence, order him
at once to confront the decree with the record of the
laws. Should he pretend not to hear you, do you
refuse to listen to him; for you are here to regard
the just defence of an honest litigant, not the subtle
apology of one who is evading the accusation. But
should he pretermit this upright course and call upon
Demosthenes, decline to receive this artisan of evil
who hopes to pervert the law by dint of words. Let
none of you, on Ctesiphon's demand, be first ready

to cry out, "Call him, call him." You call him, if you do, against yourselves, against the laws, against the Commonwealth. But if it be your pleasure to listen to Demosthenes, compel him to make his defence in the same order as the accusation] and what this is, I will recall to you.

I did not begin by going over Demosthenes's private life, nor by referring to any of his public offences, although I should have been the most inexperienced of men had I not been able to produce abundant instances of wrong from each. No! I began by exhibiting the laws which forbade the coronation of any public man whose accounts had not been passed; I then convicted Ctesiphon of having proposed a crown to Demosthenes while yet accountable, without even adding the qualifying clause "when he shall have given in his accounts," in utter disregard both of the laws and you; and I exposed the futility of the pretences set up against my case, which I now ask you to recall.

Next, I referred to the laws upon the subject of proclamations, by which it is expressly forbidden that any one crowned by the people should be so proclaimed outside of the Assembly; and I showed that the accused had not only violated the law in the first respect, but also as to the time and place of the proclamation in directing it should take place not in an Assembly but in the Theatre, not before the Athenians alone, but in the presence of all the

Greeks at the representation of the new tragedies. In conclusion I touched upon the irregularities of his private life, and expatiated at some length upon the defaults of his public career.

You should then compel Demosthenes to begin by first discussing the law relating to accountables, next as to the time and place of the proclamation, and finally, what is of most importance, to prove his title, or rather to disprove his want of title to the honor. And should he ask of you to concede to him the order and arrangement of his reply, and promise that he will answer the question of illegality at the close of his discourse, suffer him not, in ignorance of his design to deceive your tribunal, so to proceed. His purpose is not to attempt to justify the legality of the decree; and knowing that he cannot do so he will by withdrawing your attention to other matters endeavor in your possible forgetfulness of it to elude the point altogether. And as in our gymnastic sports the wrestlers skilfully contend about the choice of ground, so do you in your contest for the credit of the State strive with him the entire day if necessary to prevent his evasion of the legal points, and keeping always on your guard watch every twist and turning of his harangue, and bring him back and confine him to the real issue.

I may here foretell the part that he will play when he sees that you are in earnest in your endeavor to hold him to his true course. Ctesiphon will intro-

duce that arch-impostor, that plunderer of the public,
who has cut the constitution into shreds; the man
who can weep more easily than others laugh, and
from whom perjury flows in ready words!

He can, I doubt not, change his tone, and pass
from tears to gross abuse, insult the citizens who
are listening outside, and cry out that the partisans
of oligarchical power detected by the hand of truth
are pressing round the prosecutor to support him,
while the friends of the constitution are rallying
round the accused. And when he dares to speak
so, answer thus his seditious menaces. "What, Demosthenes, had the heroes who brought back our
fugitive citizens from Phyle been like you, our
democratic form of government had ceased to exist!
Those illustrious men saved the State exhausted by
great civil disorders in pronouncing that wise and
admirable sentence 'OBLIVION OF ALL OFFENCES.' But
you, more careful of your rounded periods than
of the City's safety, are willing to reopen all her
wounds."

When this perjurer shall seek for credit by taking
refuge in his oaths, remind him that to the forsworn
man who asks belief in them from those he has deceived so often, of two things one is needful, neither
of which exists for Demosthenes; he must either
get new Gods, or an audience not the same. And
to his tears and wordy lamentations, when he shall
ask, "Whither shall I fly, Athenians, should you cast

me out, I have not where to rest," reply, "Where shall the people seek refuge, Demosthenes; what allies, what resources, what reserve have you prepared for us? We all see what you have provided for yourself. When you have left the City, you shall not stop, as you would seem, to dwell in Piræus, but quickly thence departing, you shall visit other lands, with all the appointments for your journey provided through your corruption from Persian gold, or public plunder."

But why at all these tears, these cries, this voice of lamentation? Is it not Ctesiphon who is accused, and even for him may not the penalty be moderated by you? Thou pleadest not, Demosthenes, either for thy life, thy fortune, or thy honor!—Why is he then so disquieted? About crowns of gold, and proclamations in the Theatre against the laws:—the man who, were the people so insensate or so forgetful of the present as to wish to crown him in this time of public distress, should himself step forth and say, "Men of Athens, while I accept the crown, I disapprove the proclamation of the honor at a time like this: it should not be in regard to things for which the State is now mourning and while it is in the depth of grief."—Would not a man whose life was really upright so speak out; only a knave who assumes the garb of virtue would talk as you do?

Let none of you, by Hercules, be apprehensive lest this high-souled citizen, this distinguished warrior, from loss of this reward should on his return home take his life. The man who rates so low your consideration as to make a thousand incisions on that impure and mortgaged head which Ctesiphon proposes against all law to honor with a crown, makes money of his wounds by bringing actions for the effects of his own premeditated blows. Yes, that crown of his so often battered, that perhaps even now it bears upon it the marks of Midias's anger, that crown which brings its owner in an income, serves both for revenue and head!

Let me say a few words about this Ctesiphon the author of the decree, omitting most of what might be spoken, and touching only upon what must be apparent to you about such worthless fellows, without the aid of set phrase to assist you. I shall only mention what is common to them both and what any one might fairly say. They parade the public place expressing their opinions of each other in terms not complimentary but true. Ctesiphon tells us he has no fears about himself, for he is but a private man, but he dreads Demosthenes's venality, his cowardice, and his abject baseness. Demosthenes for his part making a self-examination has reason for great confidence, but he is worried about his friend's perversity, his shocking morals, and his odious trade of go-between! How fairly they judge themselves!—can you absolve this precious pair who know each other so well?

As for myself I briefly meet in advance the invectives which are to be launched against me. I am told that Demosthenes will insist that while the City has been well served by him on many occasions, by me it has been ever ill served. And he will fasten upon my shoulders the burthen of all the wrongs the City has endured from Philip and from Alexander. This perfidious architect of words will not be content to attack my acts of administration, and my uttered discourses; but my leisure hours, my very silence, will be slandered and accused, that no spot in my life may escape his envenomed tongue. The harmless sports of the gymnasium in the company of our youth will be misconstrued; and from the very outset of his reply he will denounce this prosecution as instituted not in the City's interest, but to pay court to Alexander, since I know so well this king loves not Demosthenes. Finally he will ask why it is that I now attack in mass the whole of his administration, when I never interfered with it or accused it in detail; why do I attack it to-day, I who never meddled with public affairs except rarely and at long intervals.

For myself, Athenians, I have neither envied the occupations of Demosthenes, nor am I ashamed of my own. I neither desire that any discourse ever made by me to you should be withdrawn, nor would I be willing to live on the condition of having to father his. My moderation, Demosthenes, has caused my silence, for my way of life is simple, I have never wished for guilty splendor. Unconstrained by any expenses, I speak or am silent as reflection dictates. But you are silent when your hands are full, and you cry out when they are empty; you speak not what or when you should, but when your paymasters exact it; and you blush not to utter boldly what the moment afterwards you are convinced was false.

This prosecution begun in Philip's lifetime, before Alexander had reached the throne, you say was brought by me to gratify the youthful king, and not in the City's behalf. But you had not then beheld the vision of Pausanias, nor had your midnight interview with Athene and with Here taken place. Could I have thus paid my court in advance to Alexander, unless I had been favored with the same dreams as Demosthenes?

You blame me for coming before the people at rare intervals, as if we were ignorant that such an argument has no place in a constitution like ours. Where the government is in the hands of a few, not who would, accuses, but he who has the power: in a democracy it is the citizen who does, and when he wills to do so. Infrequent speech before the people argues the man who speaks in their true interests and on proper occasions: the mercenary's daily harangue betrays his hire and salary for the work.

You dare to say you have never hitherto been prosecuted by me, and that you have never yet been punished for a crime! Do you presume your hearers have lost their memory, or do you deceive yourself, in recurring to such subterfuges? Perhaps you hope the people have forgotten, in the course of time, how I exposed your impious behavior about the Amphissians, and your venal conduct in the affair of Eubœa. But what time could efface the remembrance of your robberies in the matter of the triremes and the trierarchs? You introduced a law for the manning of three hundred galleys, and having persuaded the Athenians to make you Superintendent of Marine, you were convicted by me of having fraudulently withdrawn sixty-five fast-sailing cruisers, thus subtracting a larger force than that with which the City defeated the Lacedemonians and their admiral Pollis in the naval fight at Naxos.

By your recriminations against others you so embarrassed the prosecutions against yourself, that the real danger was not to you who had committed the offence, but to your accusers. Making magnificent promises for the future while you were always ruining the present, you kept pouring out abuse upon Philip and Alexander, and inveighing against others as hindering the City's opportunities. At the very moment I was about to denounce you as a State criminal, did you not contrive the arrest of Anaxinus of Oreum who was making purchases of merchandise here for Olympias, and did you not subject him to torture with your own hand, after procuring a capital sentence to be pronounced against him? Yes, this

was your treatment of the man at whose house you
had lodged, with whom you had eaten and drunk,
with whom you had made libations at the same table,
whose right hand you had clasped in yours as your
friend and host! And yet you put him to death;
and when in the face of our whole people you were
convicted of this by me, and denounced as the mur-
derer of your host, without attempting to deny it
you replied in a way that made our citizens and the
foreigners who were present cry out with indignation, that " you valued the salt of Athens more than
the table of the stranger."

I speak not now of the forged letters, the arrest
of spies and the putting of them to the torture for
pretended crimes, under the suggestion that I and
others with me were trying to make innovations in
the frame of our government. He will ask me, as I
learn, what kind of physician must he be who pre-
scribes nothing for his patient in his last illness, but
should at his funeral expatiate in presence of his
relatives upon the remedies by which he might have
been saved. But you will not ask yourself what
sort of demagogue the man is who flatters the people
to their face, but omits all occasions of saving the
Commonwealth as they occur, and by his calumnies
stays the hands of the faithful public servants who
are ready to give good counsel! You will not tell
us of the worthless minister who after involving his
country in every possible calamity deserted his post

in the hour of danger, and then demanded honors
and crowns for his services, himself the author of all
the ruin; and who after driving by his abuse from
the public service the men who might have yet saved
the State while it was possible, should insolently
demand why they had not prevented him from destroying it. And least of all will you wish to have
exposed how when after the battle we had no time
to think of your punishment while our attention was
engrossed with the safety of the State and the embassy for that purpose, it was not enough for you
that you should escape the hands of justice, but that
when by your impudent claim for rewards Athens
was made ridiculous in the sight of Greece, I was
compelled to oppose this and to bring the accusation
now under trial. But by the immortal Gods I am
most indignant, when I am told of what Demosthenes designs finally to say of me. I am like the
justly decried Sirens, it seems, and those who listen
to me, whilst they are charmed are lured on to their
destruction. My natural and acquired talents have
been used but for the injury of those who gave heed
to me. This reproach should in my opinion have
never been made against me, since it is disgraceful to
make a charge which cannot be substantiated. I can
well understand how such an accusation might have
come, not indeed from Demosthenes, but from some
rugged warrior who has performed great exploits but
is incapable of public speech, and who is naturally

jealous of the orator, when he feels that while he himself is unable to state clearly to the people his own title to esteem, the latter can even claim merit with his hearers for actions which he has never performed. But when a man who is made up of words, and those bitter and superfluous, takes refuge in a claim for simplicity of speech and the substantial merit of his conduct, who can put up with the pretensions of such a wordmonger of whom if you stop the mouth, as with a flute, there is **nothing** left?

Great will be my astonishment then to learn upon what grounds you can dismiss this prosecution. Can it be because Ctesiphon's decree is conformable to law? - Never has there been a proposition more illegal. Is it because he who has introduced it is not justly punishable for his conduct? Should you fail **to** convict him, never shall the action of a public **man** be hereafter made the subject of examination. What more melancholy spectacle than when upon a day consecrated to the honor of the State by strangers on which in the olden time the Theatre was filled with the golden crowns conferred upon the Athenian people by the other Greeks, you should not only not be crowned and proclaimed by reason of this man's policy, but that Demosthenes himself should be honored! Should any of our poets whose pieces **are** exhibited after this ceremony so far depart from truth as to represent that Thersites whom Homer has depicted as a cowardly calumniator, as crowned by the Greeks, you would rise and condemn the absurdity. And think you not if you shall undertake to crown this man, you will not be condemned and hissed in the heart of every Greek? Your fathers indeed gave to the people the credit of their own glorious achievements, and threw back upon their paltry public men what was mean and discreditable : but Ctesiphon would have you discharge Demosthenes of his own infamy that it may be fastened upon the State itself.

You proclaim that you are fortunate, as you really are, in your present prosperity. Will you by your verdict then declare that you have been abandoned by Fortune, and that you have been supported by Demosthenes alone? And grossest of inconsistencies, will you in the same tribunal in which you have condemned the guilt of those who have been convicted of bribery, honor with a crown the minister who you are convinced has allowed himself to be corrupted? In the games of our Dionysiac festivals you punish the judges for pronouncing unfairly upon the merits of the dancers. Shall you who are to decide, not upon the passing amusements of the day, but who are to judge of law, and of public virtue, award the recompense contrary to equity not to the upright deserving few, but to the factious intriguer? Then shall you the judges retire from the judgment seat belittled and enfeebled, and this orator remain all-powerful! The citizen, bear in mind, reigns in a

democratical community by the laws and by his own
vote: when he resigns to others these pledges of his
power, himself has wrought the destruction of his
own authority. The oath which he swore when he
entered upon his duties shall cease not to torment
him while he reflects upon the crime which he has
connived at; and he is even deprived of the miserable satisfaction of being known to him whom he
has favored by his perjury, since his vote was cast in
secret!

We appear, to me at least, Athenians, notwithstanding our imprudent policy, to have succeeded
sometimes in spite of our very rashness. That the
many should have abandoned to the few, in the existing juncture, the whole powers of the government,
I cannot surely approve: and yet we are fortunate
in this that the swarm of corrupt and audacious,
orators which formerly existed has not now prevailed.
Formerly indeed the republic produced many such
natures which readily overcame the people; for it
is fond of, and surrenders itself to flattery. Hence
it has been destroyed not by the men whom it distrusted, but by those upon whom it relied. Among
them were found some who ranged themselves on
the side of the Thirty Tyrants, who put to death
more than fifteen hundred citizens without trial, and
who would not even suffer their relatives to pay them
the last rites of sepulture. Will you not then shew
yourselves the masters of your public servants?

Will you not humiliate these superb orators? Will you cease to remember that never has a man in days of yore attempted the subjugation of the people, until he first proved himself to be stronger than the law and the courts of justice?

I will willingly then, Athenians, enter upon a calculation in your presence with him who drew up this decree, of the public services for which he thinks Demosthenes worthy of being crowned. Should you say, Ctesiphon,—it is the beginning of your decree, —that it is for the intrenchments with which he has surrounded the City, I admire your impudence. To have been the cause of the necessity of such works is a much heavier accusation, than to have executed them is a ground for praise. A good minister should shew his title to reward and praise not in surrounding the City with walls built from the ruins of the public tombs, but in securing to his country some substantial good. Should you pass on to the next part of your decree, in which you have dared to assert that he is a patriot who has persevered by speech and act to advance the interests of the Athenian people, lay aside the empty boast and emphasis of language, and come to the very facts, and shew us what they are. I pass over altogether those acts of venality in regard to the Amphissians and the Eubœans; but when you attribute to Demosthenes our alliance with the Thebans, you try to deceive the uninstructed, and you outrage the well-

informed. In suppressing the circumstances, in tar-
nishing the glory of your fellow-citi~~zens by~~ which
this alliance was brought about, in giving to Demosthenes the credit which belongs to the City, you attempt in vain to hide from us your malignity.

I will prove directly by a signal instance the hol-
lowness of all this pretension. The Persian king, just
before the passage of Alexander into Asia, wrote to
the people an insolent letter, in true barbaric style,
in which among other gross expressions he concluded as follows: " I shall not give you money, ask
it not, for you shall not get it." And yet this self-
same king when pressed by the dangers which menaced him, of his own accord, without demand from
us, sent over three hundred talents, which the Athenian people wisely declined to accept. It was the
time, his present fears, and the want of allies which
brought this money. And so it was with the Theban alliance. With the name of the Thebans and
with this unfortunate alliance with them you are
continually wearying us, but you keep silent about
the seventy talents of the Persian's money which you
took and diverted to your own use. And yet was it
not for want of five talents that the stranger did not
deliver up their citadel to the Thebans? Was it not
for want of nine, that when the Arcadians had taken
the field and their chiefs were disposed to come to
our assistance, the thing failed? Meanwhile you,
Demosthenes, are rich, and are revelling in every

pleasure. In a word, the Persian king's gold is with him, the dangerous Athenians, all with you.

It is well also to notice here the coarseness of these two men. Should Ctesiphon dare to call upon Demosthenes to address you iñ this cause, and he should mount the platform to deluge you with self-encomiums, their audience will be even more intolerable than the misconduct which you have endured from him. It is hard indeed to listen even to eminent men whose many actions we know to have been glorious, when they indulge in self-laudation; but it becomes insufferable when the man who sounds his own praises is a wretch who has brought disgrace upon the State.

If you are wise then, Ctesiphon, you will abstain from such scandalous conduct, but make your defence in person. You surely cannot say that you are unable to speak in public. Strange indeed would it be, if when selected with your own consent you went as a deputy to King Philip's daughter Cleopatra to present to her the condolence of the City upon the death of her husband Alexander king of the Molossians, you should now pretend that you cannot speak! You could publicly condole with a foreign princess upon her misfortune, and can you not justify a decree which you were well paid for introducing?

And can it be that he whom you have thought worthy by your decree of the honor of this crown, is so unknown to the public which has been so

largely benefited by him, that you must procure
assistance to speak in his behalf? (Ask of the
jurors whether they know Chabrias, Iphicrates, and
Timotheus, and learn from them why they have
honored and erected statues to them? Will they
not proclaim with one voice that they rendered
honor to Chabrias for his naval victory near Naxos;
to Iphicrates for having cut off a Spartan corps; to
Timotheus for his expedition to Corcyra; to other
heroes for their many glorious achievements?) Ask
them now why Demosthenes is to be rewarded. Is
it for his venality, for his cowardice, for his base
desertion of his post in the day of battle? In honoring such an one, will you not dishonor yourselves,
and the gallant men who have laid down their lives
for you in the field?—whose plaintive remonstrances
against the crowning of this man you may almost
seem to hear! Strange, passing strange, does it
seem, Athenians, that you banish from the limits
of the State the stocks and stones, the senseless im-
plements which have unwittingly caused death by
casualty;—that the hand which has inflicted the
wound of self-destruction is buried apart from the
rest of the body;—and that yet you can render
honor to this Demosthenes, by whose counsels this
last fatal expedition in which your troops were
slaughtered and destroyed was planned! The victims of this massacre are thus insulted in their
graves, and the survivors outraged and discouraged

when they behold the only reward of patriotic valor
to be an unremembered death, and a disregarded
memory! And last and most important of all con-
sequences, what answer shall you make to your
children, when they ask you after what examples
they shall frame their lives? It is not, men of
Athens, you know it well, it is not the palæstra, the
seminary, or the study of the liberal arts alone,
which form and educate our youth. Of vastly
greater value are 'the lessons taught by these honors
publicly conferred. Is a man proclaimed and crowned
in the Theatre for virtue, courage, and 'patriotism,
when his irregular and vicious life belies the honor,
the young who witness this are perverted and corrupted! Is a profligate and a pander, such as Ctesiphon, sentenced and punished, an instructive lesson
is given to the rising generation. Has a citizen voted
in opposition to justice and propriety, and does he, on
his return to his house, attempt to instruct his son;
disobedience surely follows, and the lesson is justly
looked upon as importunate and out of place. Pronounce your verdict then not as simple jurors, but
as guardians of the State, whose decision can be jus-
tified in the eyes of their absent fellow-citizens who
shall demand a strict account of it. Know ye not,
Athenians, that the people is judged by the ministers
whom it honors;—will it not be disgraceful then that
you shall be thought to resemble the baseness of
Demosthenes, and not the virtues of your ancestors?

How then is this reproach to be avoided? It must be by distrusting the men who usurp the character of upright and patriotic citizens, which their entire conduct gainsays. Good-will and zeal for the public interest can be readily assumed in name; oftentimes those who have the smallest pretensions to them by their conduct seize·upon and take refuge behind these honorable titles. When you find then an orator desirous of being crowned by strangers and of being proclaimed in presence of the Greeks, let him, as the law requires in other cases, prove the claim which he asserts by the evidence of a life free from reproach, and a wise and blameless course. If he be unable to do this, do not confirm to him·the honors.which he claims, and try at least to preserve the remnant of that public authority which is fast escaping from you. Even now, strange as it should seem, are not the Senate and the people passed over and neglected, and despatches and deputatjons received by private citizens, not from obscure individuals, but from the most important personages of Europe and Asia? Far from denying that for which under our laws the punishment is death, it is made the subject of open public boast; the correspondence is exhibited and read; and you are invited by some to look upon them as the guardians of the constitution, while others demánd to be rewarded as the saviors of the country. The people, meanwhile, as if struck with the decrepitude of age, and broken down by their misfortunes, preserve the republic only in name, and abandon to others the reality of authority. You thus retire from the Assembly, not as from a public deliberation, but as from an entertainment given at common cost where each guest carries away with him a share of the remnants of the feast. That I speak forth the words of truth and soberness, hearken to what I am about to say.

It distresses me to recur so often to our public calamities, but when a private citizen undertook to sail only to Samos to get out of the way, he was condemned to death on the same day by the Council of Areopagus as a traitor to his country. Another private citizen, unable to bear the fear which oppressed him, and sailing in consequence to Rhodes, was recently denounced for this, and escaped punishment by an equal division of the votes. Had a single one been cast on the other side, he would have been either banished or put to death. Compare these instances with the present one. An orator, the cause of all our misfortunes, who abandons his post in time of war and flies from the City, proclaims himself worthy of crowns and proclamations. Will you not drive such a man from your midst as the common scourge of Greece; or will you not rather seize upon and punish him as a piratical braggart who steers his course through our government by dint of phrases?

Consider moreover the occasion on which you are called upon to record your verdict. In a few days the Pythian Games will be celebrated, and the assembled Greeks will all be reunited in your City. She has already suffered much disparagement from the policy of Demosthenes: should you now crown him by your votes, you will seem to share the same opinions as the men who wish to break the common peace. By adopting the contrary course, you will free the State from any such suspicion.

Let your deliberations then be in accord with the interests of the City: it is for her, and not a foreign community, you are now to decide. Do not throw away your honors, but confer them with discernment upon high-minded citizens and deserving men. Search with both eyes and ears as to who they are among you who are to-day standing forth in Demosthenes's behalf. Are they the companions of his youth who shared with him the manly toils of the chase or the robust exercises of the palæstra? No, by the Olympian Jove, he has passed not his life in hunting the wild boar, or in the preparation of his body for fatigue and hardship, but in the exercise of chicane at the cost of the substance of men of wealth!

Examine well his vainglorious boasting when he shall dare to say that by his embassy he withdrew the Byzantines from the cause of Philip; that by his eloquence he detached from him the Acarnanians, and so transported the Thebans as to confirm them upon your side. He believes indeed that you have reached such a point of credulity that you are ready to be persuaded by him of anything he may choose to utter, as if you had here in your midst the goddess Persuasion herself, and not an artful demagogue.

And when at the close of his harangue Demosthenes shall invite the partakers of his corruption to press round and defend him, let there be present in your imagination upon the platform from which I am now speaking the venerable forms of the ancient benefactors of the State arrayed in all their virtue to oppose these men's insolence. I see among them the wise Solon, that upright law-giver who founded our popular government upon the soundest principles of legislation, gently advising you with his native moderation not to place your oaths and the law under the control of this man's discourse. And Aristides, by whose equity the imposts upon the Greeks were regulated, whose daughters left in poverty through his incorruptible integrity were endowed by the State, Aristides is seen complaining of this outrage upon justice, and demanding whether the descendants of the men who thought worthy of death and actually banished from their City and country Arthmius the Zelian then living in their midst and enjoying the sacred rights of hospitality for merely bringing Persian gold into Greece, are now going to cover themselves with disgrace by honoring with a crown of gold the man who has not simply brought hither the stranger's money, but is enjoying here the price of his treason. And Themistocles and the men who fell at Marathon and Platæa, think you that they are insensible to what is taking place! Do not their voices cry out from the very tombs in mournful protest against this perverse rendering of honor to one who has dared to proclaim his union with the barbarians against the Greeks!

As for me, Oh Earth and Sun, oh Virtue, and thou, Intelligence, by whose light we are enabled to discern and to separate good from evil, as for me, I have directed my efforts against this wrong, I have lifted up my voice against this injustice! If I have spoken well and loftily against this crime, I have spoken as I could have wished; but if my utterances have been feeble and ill-directed, still they have been according to the measure of my strength. It is for you, men of Athens and jurors, to weigh carefully both what has been spoken and what has been left unsaid, and to render such a decision as shall not only be upright but for the advantage of the State.

DEMOSTHENES

ON BEHALF OF

CTESIPHON.

DEMOSTHENES ON BEHALF OF CTESIPHON.

FIRST of all, Athenians, I implore of the Gods and Goddesses, that the same good-will which I feel and have ever shewn to the City and to all of you shall be shewn by you to me in this contest. Next,—this concerns you especially, your piety and glory,—that they may inspire you not to suffer my antagonist to control you as to the manner in which you shall hear my defence, (this would indeed be cruel,) but that in this you will keep before you the law and your oath, in which, among other proper things, this also is prescribed, that YOU SHALL REGARD BOTH SIDES EQUALLY. And this means not only that you shall not forejudge anything, not merely that you shall shew the same good-will to both sides, but that you shall permit each party to adopt freely that arrangement and course of argument in his address which he may prefer and think most convenient.

In many things, indeed, am I at a disadvantage with Æschines in this encounter;—in two matters

of great importance, in particular. We are by no
means equal in this;—it is not the same thing to me
if I shall forfeit your good-will, to him if he merely
fails in the prosecution:—to me, indeed—but I dare
not in the outset of my reply say anything of ill
omen. My opponent therefore accuses me at his
ease. Again, men by their constitution hear readily
attacks and abuse of others, but listen with disgust
to all self-panegyric. What is agreeable, therefore,
falls to his part; to me is left, so to speak, what
is distasteful to all to hear. On the one hand then,
if in the fear of thus offending I omit to speak of
what has been done by me, I may seem to fail to
answer the charges brought against me, and not to
shew for what I am entitled to honor; on the other
hand, if I enter upon my course of action and my
policy, I shall be often compelled to speak of myself.
I shall endeavor, however, to do this with as much
reserve as possible; but for so much as I shall be
forced to say, it is proper to hold him responsible
who has instituted this prosecution.

Men of Athens and jurors, I think you will all
admit that this contest concerns me as much as
Ctesiphon, and deserves no less earnest attention
from my hands than from his. For, to be deprived
of anything, especially by an enemy, is grievous and
hard to bear, but to lose your good opinion and
your affection is the greatest of misfortunes, as their
possession is the most inestimable blessing.

Such being the nature of the controversy, I beseech
you all alike to listen to my defence to this accusation with the fairness which the laws require. Those
laws, established long ago by Solon, who was your
well-wisher and a friend of the people, were thought
by him not only to be binding by reason of their inscription, but because you were sworn to observe
them. Not that, as it seems to me, he distrusted you
in so causing you to be sworn, but that he foresaw
that the accused could never escape the enmities and
malice in which the strength of the prosecutor, from
being allowed to speak first, lies, unless each one of
the jury, guarding his probity by an appeal to the
Gods, should listen favorably and justly to what
should be asserted by the defence, and in the same
spirit of impartiality to both sides enter upon an
examination of the whole cause.

Since I am about to give, then, as it would seem,
an account as well of my whole private life as of my
public career, I desire, as in the outset, to appeal
again to the immortal Gods; and in presence of you
all, I implore them first to direct you to show to me
in this contest the same kindness which I have ever
felt to you and to your city; next, that they will inspire you so to pass upon this prosecution as shall
redound to your common credit, and to the elevation
of the character of each one of you.

Had Æschines merely followed in the line of his
attack the matters upon which he has founded the

prosecution, I could have readily defended the preliminary decree; but since he has, in unmeasured speech, gone over many other things, scattering the foulest abuse upon me, it is necessary and proper that I should first briefly reply to these, lest some of you, led astray by such foreign matters, might hear me with disfavor upon the merits of the charge itself.

See how fairly and directly I shall answer all that this man has so slanderously alleged against my private life. If you have known me to be such as he accuses me,—and I have lived my whole life among you,—permit not my voice to be heard, no matter how well I have managed public affairs, but rise and condemn me on the spot. If, on the other hand, you believe and know me to be better and of better descent than my accuser, and—not to speak too presumptuously—that I and mine are inferior to no respectable citizens, then disregard everything which he has said about my public life, since it will be apparent he has falsified in everything. I shall only ask you to shew me now the same kindness which you have always shewn in the past in the many contests in which I have been engaged. But malicious as you are, Æschines, you must be very simple to think I shall now pass by all that you have said about my political course, and begin by taking up your abuse of my private character. I shall do nothing of the kind. I am not quite so absurd. I shall first notice your falsehoods and slanders about my public life; and afterwards touch upon the scurrilous abuse you have been pouring out so freely upon me, should the jurors wish to hear me about it.

The charges which have been made are many and astounding, and to some of them the laws affix severe and even the greatest punishments; but the management of this prosecution presents all the abuse and insulting conduct of a private enemy, the malice, the contumelious treatment, and all its characteristics. If the charges and accusations brought are true, the City can never take sufficient vengeance for them, or anything like it. It is most unseemly therefore to prevent the person accused from appealing to the people and exercising his right of speech before them; but to act thus in the interest of private enmity and malice, by the Gods, Athenians, I hold to be unconstitutional as well as most unrighteous and unjust. If Æschines has known me to be guilty of deliberate breaches of the law against the City, were they as enormous as he has been charging and declaiming, the penalties affixed to them by the laws should have been awarded. If he has seen me doing acts which deserved impeachment, he should have impeached me and brought me to trial before you for them. If my conduct has been unconstitutional, it should have been so proved and punished. But he should not pursue Ctesiphon for me: for had he thought he could have convicted me, he certainly would never have brought an accusation against him.

Besides, had he seen me committing any of the crimes which he has just been falsely accusing me of and charging upon me, or any other offences against you, for all such there were laws, and punishments, and trials, and judgments, with sharp and severe penalties : all these it was open to him to employ against me ; and had he been found doing this, had he made use of this method against me, his charges would at least have been consistent with his actions.   Now, however, he has turned aside from the honest and direct path, and avoiding at the time to confront the allegations with the proofs, he is playing a part by heaping up at this late day accusations, and calumnies, and ribaldry.

Furthermore, he is attacking ME, whilst he is prosecuting Ctesiphon, making his hatred of me the head and front of the whole contest; and not fairly meeting me even on this ground, he is endeavoring to take away the privileges of another.   Thus in addition to all the arguments, Athenians, which may be brought forward in favor of Ctesiphon, this it seems to me may also be strongly urged, that it is proper that the inquiry into our private griefs should be made between ourselves, and that we should not quit our personal quarrel, to find out how much punishment we can inflict upon a third person; this were the height of injustice.

Any one can see then from what I have said, how all that he has brought against me is devoid of truth and justice. But I wish to examine the charges separately, and in particular what he has falsely accused me of in regard to the peace and the embassy, which was really done by himself in concert with Philocrates. It is necessary and right to do this, that you may have brought to your recollection what actually took place at that time, so that you can look at each event in its proper order.

When the Phocian war broke out, (not caused by me,—I was not then in public life,) you were at first in this position; although you knew the Phocians had acted improperly, yet you desired them to be saved from ruin; and as you had just cause of irritation against the Thebans, you would even have been pleased at their suffering any reverse; for they had used their success at Leuctra immoderately. Besides, all Peloponnesus was at variance with itself. Neither those who hated the Lacedemonians were strong enough to crush them; nor were those who by the Spartans' means had at first triumphed able to remain masters of the Cities. Everywhere secret enmity, strife and trouble prevailed,—not only there, but throughout all the States. All this was manifest to Philip, (indeed it was plain enough,) and he scattered his bribes freely to traitors in every city in order to set the Greeks by the ears; and by introducing confusion and hatred among them he took advantage of their blunders and dissensions, and grew in strength to their common detriment.

The Thebans,—then insolent enough, now alas so unfortunate,—worn out by the length of the war, were manifestly compelled to turn to you; but Philip, anxious to prevent this and to keep the cities apart, offered peace to you and aid to them. Why was he so near taking you as willing captives by his seductive arts? It was through the baseness, or the folly, —or call it both,—of the other Greeks. While you had been carrying on a long and incessant war for the common benefit of all, as the result plainly shewed, they never assisted you in the least, either by money, by troops, or in any way. Justly and naturally displeased with this, you listened readily to Philip. The peace that was concluded was thus brought about in this way,—not through me, as Æschines has falsely asserted. The cause, then, of our present condition, any one who shall fairly inquire will find in the criminality and corruption of these men at the time of the treaty.

All this I have accurately recounted for the sake of truth. If anything seems wrong in it, it is surely nothing to me. The first man who spoke of or called your attention to peace was Aristodemus, the actor; he who came next and wrote the decree, hired by Philip for the purpose equally with the other, was Philocrates, the Agnusian,—YOUR accomplice, Æschines, not MINE,—though you should burst with falsely asserting this, I say it. Their supporters, whatever were their motives, (I pass this by for the

present,) were Eubulus and Kephisophon. I had
nothing to do with it. But although this was so,
as has just been clearly shewn, he has nevertheless
reached this height of effrontery as to assert boldly
that I was the author of the peace, and that I prevented the City from concluding it with the Common
Council of the Greeks. Oh, you!—How can any
one rightly characterize you? If you were present
and saw me depriving the City of this fine thing, this
alliance as grand as you now style it, why did you
not express your indignation, why did you not come
forward and proclaim and expose what you are now
denouncing me for? And if, in Philip's pay, I was
defeating the common interests of Greece, you should
not have then sat silent, but you should have thun-
dered, and protested against it, and proclaimed it to
all. You then did nothing of the kind; no one ever
heard that voice of yours. And for a good reason,
Athenians. No embassy was sent by you to any of
the Greeks; they had all long before declared themselves. Æschines has told nothing true about this.

Moreover, in all that he has said he has chiefly
slandered the City. For had you invited the other
Greeks into this war, and had then sent ambassadors
to Philip to treat of peace, your conduct would have
been that of Eurybatus, unworthy of the City, or of
honorable men. But it is not, it is not so. Why
should you have sent to the Greeks at that time?
To treat of peace? All then had it. To discuss

war? But you were then deliberating about peace.
It is plain that I was neither the author of the peace,
nor even advocated it; nor has any of his other false
charges against me been shewn to be true.

Peace being then concluded, let us see what part
each of us took, that you may thence understand
who was working in everything for Philip, and who
was active in your behalf eagerly on the lookout for
what might be useful to the City. It was then that
I wrote the decree directing the ambassadors to sail
without delay to wheresoever Philip might be, and to
receive the oaths from him. They would not, however, act in accordance with this. The value of the
decree I will explain.

It was Philip's interest to delay the taking of the
oaths as long as he could, whilst it was yours to have
it done as soon as possible, and for this reason. From
the very day not only on which you had sworn to the
peace, but from the time you had hoped it might be
obtained, you had laid aside all preparation for war.
Philip, on the contrary, had from that moment re-
doubled his efforts, convinced, as it really turned out,
that whatever he might deprive the City of, he should
be able to retain firmly, as no one would be disposed
to give up peace on that account. I foresaw this,
Athenians, and carefully weighing the matter, I prepared the decree requiring them to sail to where Philip
was, and there at once receive the oaths from him.
The oaths were to be so taken, that the Thracians

your allies should still retain the places which Æs-chines now belittles—Serrium, Myrtium, and Ergiske —and that Philip should not seize the principal posts, and thus becoming master of all Thrace, draw from it resources and troops, and be readily enabled to accomplish his further purposes.

Æschines neither reads this decree nor notices it, but attacks me because when Senator I advised that it was proper to receive Philip's envoys. But what was to be done? To decree that after coming hither they should not be admitted to confer with you? Or was the manager of the Theatre to be ordered not to furnish them seats? For two oboli they could have purchased them in spite of a decree. Would it have been well in me to have watched over these petty interests of the City, and to have betrayed its im-portant ones, as these men did? By no means. Read now the decree which this man has purposely ignored.

DECREE.

"In the archonship of Mnesiphilus, on the last day of Heca-tombeon, during the presidency of the tribe Pandion, Demosthe-nes, son of Demosthenes of Pæania, moved, that whereas Philip had sent ambassadors to treat of peace with us upon certain stipulated conditions, it should be decreed by the Council and people of Athens that for the purpose of ratifying the peace which had been agreed upon in the first Assembly, five ambassa-dors chosen from all the Athenians should proceed without delay to meet Philip wheresoever he might be, and there exchange oaths with him as speedily as possible upon the terms agreed upon between him and the Athenian people, the allies on both sides being included in the treaty. The ambassadors chosen are Eubulus, of Anaphlystus; Æschines, of Cothocidæ; Kephisophon, of Rhamnus; Democrates, of Phlyus; and Cleon, of Cothocidæ."

This decree had been prepared by me in the City's interest, not in Philip's; but our precious envoys, utterly disregarding it, sat down three whole months in Macedonia, until Philip had left Thrace after reducing it entirely to submission. In ten days—even in three or four—they could have reached the Hellespont, and saved these places, by receiving the oaths from him before he had captured them. He could never have touched them had we been present;—certainly we should not have received the oaths from him; he would have missed the peace, or he could not have held on to both the peace and these posts.

This was Philip's first perfidy, the purchase, in the matter of the embassy, of these abominable men, accursed of the Gods. For this I was then, am now, and ever shall be their enemy and opponent. But you shall see immediately after this a still greater piece of villainy. Philip having at last taken the oaths, but not until he had made himself master of Thrace through the disobedience of these men to my decree, obtained from them for a price that they should not quit Macedonia until he had everything ready for his expedition against the Phocians. He feared that if they should let you know what he was

preparing to do, you might sail with your fleet to
Thermopylæ and close the Straits, as you had formerly done; he hoped, therefore, you would receive
no intelligence until he was fairly there, and then
you could do nothing.

But Philip was in fear and mortal agony lest, after
he had taken the pass, you might still resolve to aid
the Phocians before he had destroyed them, and the
thing should thus slip through his hands. So he
bribes this miserable creature, not in the lump with
the other envoys, but singly by himself, to announce
to you propositions by giving heed to which everything might be ruined. I call upon you, Athenians,
to remember, and I beg of you to keep it in
mind throughout the whole of this trial, that if
Æschines had not himself travelled out of the
record to load me with abuse, I should never have
uttered a single word foreign to it. But to all the
accusations and assaults which he has so freely made
against me, I must absolutely reply a little by way of
answer to the various charges contained in them.

What was it, then, that was announced to you by
him, which caused this entire ruin?—"That you
need not be uneasy because Philip had passed the
Straits; for everything would turn out as you wished,
if you would only keep quiet; and in two or three
days you would find out that he would prove the
friend of those against whom he was marching as an
enemy, and the enemy of those to whom he seemed

friendly. It was not words," said he, talking in his solemn manner, "but a community of interest that really cemented friendship. Your interest and Philip's and the Phocians' were the same,—to free yourself from the insolence and heavy oppressiveness of the Thebans."

All this was received with satisfaction by many of you on account of the secret dislike felt against the Thebans. What took place soon afterwards? It was not long in coming.—The Phocians were destroyed; their cities annihilated. You who had waited patiently, relying upon this fellow, were in a little while compelled to bring in all your effects from the country to the city, Æschines pocketed his pay, and besides, the hatred of the Thebans and Thessalians was transferred to you, and their gratitude to Philip for what had taken place. To prove that this is so, I shall have now read to you the decree of Calisthenes and Philip's letter, which will make all as plain as daylight. Read them:

DECREE.

"In the archonship of Mnesiphilus, at a special Assembly convened by the generals with the advice of the Senators and Council, on the twenty-first day of Mæmacterion, Calisthenes, son of Eteonicus of Phalerum, moved that no Athenian should under any pretext pass the night in the country, but that all should remain in the city and in Piræus, except such as were distributed in the garrisons; that these last should maintain their posts, neither quitting them by day or night; that any one disobeying should be punished as a traitor unless he could shew the impossibility of obedience, the cause of disobedience to be decided by the generals of arms and superintendence of finance, assisted by the clerk of the Senate. All property should be brought as speedily as possible from the country into the city, and into Piræus, if the distance did not exceed one hundred and twenty stadia;* beyond that distance, into Eleusis, Phyle, Aphidna, Rhamnus, and Sunium. Calisthenes of Phalerum has so moved."

Was this the hope with which you made peace; or was this the promise which this hireling held out to you?

Read now the letter which Philip sent you after all was done.

LETTER.

"Philip, king of Macedon, to the Council and People of Athens, Greeting:—Know that I have passed Thermopylæ and reduced Phocis to subjection. In such of their towns as have at once submitted I have placed garrisons; those which have resisted I have taken by force, razed to the ground, and sold their inhabitants into slavery. As I have learned that you were preparing to assist them, I now write to you that you may save yourselves the trouble. You seem, in fine, to be acting altogether unreasonably in your intention of marching against me while you are still at peace with me,—and for the Phocians, too, who are not included in our treaties. Should you fail to stand by our mutual obligations you will gain nothing more than to be the first to commit injustice."

See how plainly in this letter to you he discloses

---

* A stadium is a little less than a furlong.

himself, and speaks to his allies. "I have done this," says he, "in spite of the Athenians, and to their great annoyance; if you are wise, Thebans and Thessalians, you will look upon them as your enemies, and trust entirely to me." He does not, it is true, use these very words, but this is what he designs to convey. In this manner he so got the mastery of them, that they foresaw, they perceived nothing, and allowed him ever after to manage everything in his own way. Hence all the disasters which the wretched Thebans have suffered. But he who was the fellow-worker with Philip, and, with him, the cause of this confidence, he who announced falsehoods to you, and altogether deceived you, this is the man who is now pitying the miseries of the Thebans, giving their sad detail, himself the author of all the calamities of the Phocians, and of whatever else the Greeks have been afflicted with. It is very plain that you, Æschines, are mourning over what has happened, and are compassionating the Thebans, you, who possess their property, and are cultivating their fields in Bœotia; while I, forsooth; am rejoicing over it, I, who was at once demanded to be delivered up by the originator of all this ruin!

But I am touching upon matters which it will be more fitting to speak of a little later. I return now to shew that the iniquity of these men was the cause of all our present disasters.

After you had been thus cheated in the embassy by

Philip through these men who had been, purchased by him to report nothing truly to you, after the unhappy Phocians had been cheated and their cities had been destroyed, what next occurred? The contemptible Thessalians and the besotted Thebans regarded Philip as their friend, benefactor, and savior. He was all in all to them. They would not hear a word against this. You, however, who were much annoyed at what had taken place, and naturally distrustful, still kept the peace; indeed there was nothing else you could have done alone. The other Greeks, tricked like yourselves, and disappointed in their hopes, willingly kept the peace too, although in a certain sense all had been for a long time attacked by him. For when Philip in his hostile movements had overcome the Illyrians and Triballians, besides destroying some of the Grecian cities, in this way mightily increasing his power and resources; and when many of these vile men, some from every city, Æschines among the rest, had repaired to his Court, under the pretext of the peace, to receive the wages of corruption, all the States against which Philip had been manœuvring, he was really making war upon. If they did not see this, that was another affair, and no fault of mine. I spoke out and I testified both at home and wherever I was sent by you, in season and out of season. But the States of Greece were in the lethargy of disease; the men at the head of affairs had been bribed by largesses; of the citizens, some closed their eyes to what was going on, others were allured by the bait of a present life of easy indifference;—all were afflicted with the same malady. They believed the impending blow would not fall upon their heads, and some actually thought they could, when they wished, find their own safety in the ruin of their neighbors. It happened, I fancy, that while the people lost their liberties from preferring to them an inglorious ease, their leaders who thought they were selling every one but themselves, found they were the first who were betrayed. Instead of friends and guests,—the names bestowed upon them while they were being purchased,—they were called parasites, enemies of the Gods, and such like names, when they were no longer serviceable. And justly. —For no one, Athenians, thinks of the interests of the corrupt man when he is bribing him, or continues to take the advice of a traitor after he has become master of what he has been buying from him. Nothing would be pleasanter than a traitor's life were this so: but it is not;—very far from it. When he who is striving for the mastery reaches the height of power, and becomes the lord of the betrayers, that moment he sees through all their villainy, and hates, and mistrusts, and loathes them. Consider this; if the time of action be past, the time for looking at things as they really are. is at least always present to the wise man. Lasthenes was thus called Philip's friend until he betrayed Olynthus to him, and no longer. And Timolaus, until he ruined Thebes. So also Eudicus and Simus the Larissians, until they had placed Thessaly at Philip's feet. After this, the world was filled with these traitors, driven away, insulted, and a prey to every evil. How did Aristratus fare in Sikyon, and Perilaus in Megara? Were they not outcasts? From all this it is plain, Æschines, that he who cherishes his country, and is ever opposed to such men as you, really enables the traitor and the venal statesman to trade upon their corruption; for it is through the people, and the men who are opposed to your designs, that you continue safe and purchasable; you would have long since been ruined by your own conduct.

I had still much more to say about these matters, but perhaps I have said too much already. This man, however, is the cause of it; as he has been pouring out upon me the dregs of his vile abuse and injustice, it was necessary I should defend myself against it with the younger portion of my hearers, who are new to what took place so long ago. You are all doubt- less now weary of it, since you must have been con- vinced of his having been in Philip's pay before I said a word upon the subject. He calls it friendship and intimacy, and speaking of me in connection with it a little while ago, he said, "He finds fault with my intimacy with Alexander."—I talk of your intimacy with Alexander! How did you obtain it, and what is your title to it? I never called you the friend of

11

Philip, or the intimate of Alexander. I have not quite lost my senses. You might as well speak of the reapers and hired laborers as the friends and guests of their employers. But this is impossible. I did call you the hireling first of, Philip, and afterwards of Alexander; and all who are listening know it is so. If you doubt it, ask them; or rather I will do it for you. Athenians, which is Æschines, Alexander's hired man, or his friend?—You hear their answer.

I now desire, however, to answer the charge itself, and to speak in detail about my public life. Æschines already knows it, but he shall hear from what I say that I happen to be not only deserving of the honors which were decreed to me, but of rewards very much greater. Read the accusation.

ACCUSATION.

"In the archonship of Chærondas, on the sixth day of Elaphebolion, Æschines, son of Atrometus, of Cothocidæ, lodged with the Archon an accusation against Ctesiphon, son of Leosthenes, the Anaphlystian, for that contrary to law he has brought forward a decree providing that Demosthenes, son of Demosthenes the Pæanian, shall be crowned with a golden crown, proclamation to be made in the Theatre during the Dionysiac festivals while the new tragedies are being performed, that the people crown the aforesaid Demosthenes with a golden crown as a reward for his virtue and the good-will which he has ever displayed towards all the Greeks and the people of Athens in particular, and for his excellence in speech and action in behalf of the true interests of the people, and his zeal in doing the best that could be done; all of which was decreed by him falsely and contrary to law ; the laws in the first place forbidding falsehoods to be injected into the public records; next, it being unlawful to vote a crown to a person whose accounts have not been passed, the said Demosthenes being still a Commissioner for the erection of walls, and Administrator of the Theoric fund; and lastly, it being contrary to law that the crowning of any one should be proclaimed at the Theatre during the Dionysiac festivals at the time of the new tragedies, it being required that if a crown be voted by the Council, proclamation thereof shall be made in the Council Chamber, and if by the City, at the Pnyx during the holding of an Assembly. The fine incurred is fifty talents. Witnesses, Kephisophon, son of Kephisophon, of Rhamnus; Cleon, son of Cleon, of Cothocidæ."

This is what is charged, Athenians, against the decree. From the language of the charge itself, I think I shall make it clear to you that I shall be able to answer it successfully. I shall pursue the same order as that of the accusation, and meet every specification in detail, omitting nothing purposely.

As the decree commends me for having always, by word and deed, acted for the true interest of Athens, and for having zealously accomplished the best that was in my power, I necessarily regard my public life, as placed in issue. From a careful review of it it will then be found whether Ctesiphon, in proposing what he did, spoke truly or falsely. And as he did not direct that the coronation was to take place after I had given in my accounts; and as it was ordered to be done in the theatre, I think it equally plain that this referred also to my public career, and whether I was deserving or not of this honor, and of its being proclaimed in the manner mentioned. I deem it however proper to produce the laws under which Ctesiphon was authorized to decree as he did. I shall then, men of Athens, make my defence fairly and frankly in this way, and go over my public life at some length. And let no one suppose I shall be departing from the scope of the accusation should I touch upon matters relating to the affairs of Greece. In attacking the decree as untruly stating that I did not advise and perform what was best for my country, the propounder of the charge has made my whole policy pertinent and even necessary to its discussion. And as upon my entrance into public life I made choice of the department of the affairs of Greece, from this quarter also I am entitled to draw my proofs.

I pass by altogether what Philip had gotten and held before I began to speak and to take part in affairs; with this, I think, I have no concern. But from the day on which I undertook to act a part, in what way I was able to resist his plans I shall mention in detail, first premising, however, as follows. Philip had one enormous advantage in this, that throughout Greece, not here and there but everywhere, there was a swarm of traitors and corrupt men, detested of the Gods, such as theretofore no one could recollect having ever seen. These men he made use of as co-workers in his purpose, and what was at first bad enough in the conduct of the Greeks towards each other, he made much worse by deceiving some, purchasing others, and corrupting all in various ways. He thus divided them into an hundred parties when there should have been but a single purpose in them all,—to resist his growing greatness. In this conjuncture, and in ignorance of the existing and increasing evil by the other Greeks, it becomes us to consider what was proper for the City to do, and to hold me responsible for what was actually done. For it was I who settled its policy in this respect.

Was the City, Æschines, to abjure its pride and dignity, and to imitate the Thessalians and Dolopians in helping Philip to obtain the headship of Greece, and thus to set at nought the wise and glorious precedents of our ancestors? Or if she abstained from doing this,—this would indeed have been shameful, —after foreseeing from afar what would inevitably take place unless resisted, was she to disregard it altogether? And here I would willingly ask the most envious carper at what has been done, which side he would have wished the City to embrace,—to be an instrument in bringing about the calamities and disgraces which befell Greece, as the Thessalians and those who worked with them were, or to ignore totally what was taking place in the hope of purchasing their own security, as we saw the Arcadians and Mes-

senians and Argives do? Yet most of these States,
or in fact all of them, suffered more than we.—Had
Philip, indeed, after his success, thought proper to
retrace his steps, and to remain quiet, neither perse-
cuting his allies nor the other Greeks, there might
have been grounds for the accusation which has been
brought against the opponents of his policy. But
when he was aiming to strike down not only the
glory, the power, the liberties of our people, but their
very institutions themselves só far as he could, can it
be possible that in following my advice you have not
pursued the most honorable course?

But I return to this.—What did it behoove the
City, Æschines, to do when it saw Philip preparing
to obtain the command and empire of Greece?
What did it become me, a Counsellor of Athens, to
advise by words or by decrees, (this is the vital
point,)—I, who knew my country had always, from
the earliest times down to the very hour I first ascended the platform, been striving for the highest
place in honor and glory, and with a noble emulation
had spent more treasure and given more lives to
assist Greece than all the Greeks together had done
to assist themselves?—I, who saw this very Philip,
with whom you were contending for leadership and
mastery, with one eye gone, his shoulder shattered,
maimed of a hand and leg, yet freely abandoning to
fortune whatever else she wanted of his body, if he
might only live glorious and honored with what was

left? Not only this, but that any one should dare to
say that such a height of arrogance could enter the
breast of a man reared at Pella—a little spot unknown
to Fame—as to aspire to or even conceive of attain-
ing to the command of Greece; and that such abject
baseness was yours, Athenians, who saw each day, in
every word uttered, and in every spectacle around
you, the memorials of your ancestors' virtue,—that
you could abandon, that you could voluntarily give
up to Philip· the liberties of Greece!—Impossible
that any one should say this! You were then all
bound to oppose this man's injustice by every just
means. And you fairly and willingly assumed this
from the start; and I counselled, and I wrote decrees, and I contrived according to my ability
throughout all this time. But what was the best
thing to be done?

I ask you again;—put aside Amphipolis, Pydna,
Potidæa, Halonnesus, and the rest,—I make no mention of them. And so also as to Serrium, Doriscus,
and the destruction of Peparethus, and whatever else
the country was injured in;—I care not if they took
place. And yet you have said that it was I who, in
advising as to these things, precipitated the Athenians
into hostility with Philip, when in reality the decrees
were written by Eubulus and Aristophon and Dio-
pithes, not by me. Oh reckless utterer of whatever
you choose to say!—I will not now, however, speak
of these things.—But when Philip appropriated Eu-

bœa to himself, making use of it as an objective point against Attica, and laid his hands upon Megara, and captured Oreus, and destroyed Porthmus, and on the one side established Philistides as tyrant in Oreus, and on the other Clitarchus in Eretria, and reduced the Hellespont under his control, and besieged Byzantium, and took possession of some Grecian cities, and put back in others the fugitives from them,—was the man who did all this, acting with injustice? And was he setting his engagements at nought? And did he break the peace or not? And was it proper that any Grecian State should try to prevent all this? If it was not, but it was right that Greece should become a Mysian prey, the Athenians strong and powerful looking on meanwhile, then I wasted my breath in speaking as I did, and the City wasted its time in paying attention to me, and all that was done by me was a blunder and a wrong. But if it was right for any of the Grecian States to interfere to prevent all this, then was not Athens the proper party to do it? I did direct all my measures to this end; I did oppose this man, whom I saw attempting to enslave every people; and both by my words and by my teachings I did advise you not to permit all Greece to be delivered into his hands. I admit all this.

It was not the City, however, Æschines, which broke the peace; it was Philip, by taking our ships. Bring forward the decrees and Philip's letter, and

read them consecutively; it will then be apparent
who was the cause of this.

DECREE.

"In the archonship of Neocles, in the month Boedromion, at
an extraordinary Assembly convened by the generals, Eubulus,
son of Mnesitheus, of Coprus, moved that whereas the generals
had announced to the Assembly that Leodamas, our admiral,
and twenty ships under his command, which had been sent to
the Hellespont for the transport of corn, had been carried off by
Amyntas, Philip's general, to Macedonia, and there kept under
guard, the senators and generals should provide that a council
be called to choose deputies to be sent to Philip to ask the re-
lease of our admiral and ships and sailors. And if it shall
appear that Amyntas has done this through ignorance, the
Athenians find no fault with him. Or if it be alleged that he
captured Leodamas because he was transgressing his orders, the
Athenians will examine into it, and punish him according to
the measure of his offence. But if neither of these things be
the cause, and the wrong has been done by the orders either of
Philip or his lieutenant, then the deputies shall report this, so
that the people may consider the matter and advise as to what
ought to be done."

This decree was written by Eubulus, not by me.
And then came Aristophon with another, and Hege-
sippus with his, then Aristophon again, then Philocrates, then Kephisophon, then all the others with
theirs. But I proposed none. Read again.

DECREE.

"In the archonship of Neocles, on the last day of Boedromion,
the senators and generals brought and submitted to the opinion

of the Council the decree of the Assembly that it had seemed proper to the people that deputies should be sent to Philip in regard to the return of our ships, and that instructions be given to them according to the tenor of the Assembly's decree. The following persons were chosen: Kephisophon, son of Cleon, the Anaphlystian; Democritus, son of Demophon, the Anagyrasian; Polycritus, son of Apemantes, the Cothocidian. In the presidency of the tribe Hippothoontis, Aristophon, of Collytta, moving the decree."

I have now produced these decrees, and do you, Æschines, if you can, produce any which I wrote which caused the war. You cannot. If you could you would have been ready enough with it. Even Philip never accused me of this, blaming others as the authors of the war. Read Philip's letter now.

LETTER.

"Philip, King of Macedon, to the Council and people of Athens, Greeting. The deputies sent by you to me, Kephisophon, and Democritus, and Polycritus, have complained about the capture of your ships under the command of Leodamas. You seem to me to be very simple if you think I am ignorant that your sending these ships to transport corn from the Hellespont to Lemnos was a pretext, it being in reality to assist the Selymbrians who were besieged by me and who were not included in our common treaties of friendship. And this was done without the knowledge of the people by your admiral acting under the orders of certain men who control your affairs and of others not now in office but who desire in every way, notwithstanding our existing friendship, that you should be at war with me, being much more anxious to bring this about than to aid the Selymbrians, and because they also believe they would make profit out of it. It seems to me, however, it will neither be of service to you nor to me. I return your ships to you, and if for the future you will not suffer the men at the head of affairs to advise you badly but will disgrace them, I on my part will endeavor to preserve the peace. Farewell."

In no manner, you see, did he accuse Demosthenes, nor in any way inculpate him. Why was it, then, that when he was finding fault with all the others, he made no reference to anything which had been done by me? Because in attacking me he would have brought forward the remembrance of his own injustice. Those acts of wrong I had always set myself against, those perfidies I had always opposed. When Philip first stole into Peloponnesus, I sent thither an embassy; so also did I to Euboea, when he was trying to pounce upon that island; and when he was endeavoring to establish tyrants in Oreus and Eretria, I sent thither no embassies, but military expeditions. I then despatched the fleets by which Chersonnesus, Byzantium, and all our allies were saved.

In consequence of this, there flowed in upon you from the States which you had thus relieved, praise, glory, honors, crowns, thanks, the highest commendations. Of those who had been wronged and who had heeded your advice the safety was assured; those who had neglected to follow what you had so often tried to impress upon them, now found out that you had not only been well disposed to them, but came to look upon you as wise and far-seeing men: everything fell out as you had predicted. What would not Philistides have given to have kept Oreus, or Clitarchus to have kept Eretria, or Philip, himself, to have had these cities under his control, so that he could use them against you;—to have had no one to call him to account for his other misdeeds, no censor to overlook and control him in his acts of injustice? No one feels any doubt as to this, and nobody less than you, Æschines. For the envoys who were sent hither by Philistides and Clitarchus took up their quarters with you, you were their host. When the City dismissed them as enemies who were proposing unjust things, you stood their friend. But none of those things was done, calumniator of my conduct, who assert that I am silent when my hands are full, but that I cry out when they are empty! You, on the contrary, cry out when your hands are full; and will never cease until your fellow-citizens shall stop your mouth by a sentence of disgrace. It was then that you, my fellow-citizens, crowned me for what I had done, and Aristonicus wrote the decree in the self-same words which Ctesiphon has used in the present one. The proclamation was ordered to be made in the Theatre; and although I received the honor for the second time, and Æschines was present, he brought no accusation against the mover of the decree. Read it here.

DECREE.

"In the archonship of Chærondas, son of Hegemon, on the twenty-fifth day of Gamelion, during the presidency of the tribe Leontis, Aristonicus of Phrearrii moved that Demosthenes, son of Demosthenes of Pæania, having rendered many and great services to the Athenian people, and heretofore to many of their allies, and having at the present time aided them by decrees, and brought about the freedom of certain cities in Eubœa, and having persevered in his good-will to the City, and said and done what was best for the Athenians and all the Greeks, it be decreed by the Council and people of Athens that the said Demosthenes be publicly praised and crowned with a golden crown, and that the crown be conferred upon him in the Theatre at the Dionysiac festivals, at the representation of the new tragedies. The presiding tribe and the Master of the Games shall take charge of the proclamation. Aristonicus of Phrearrii has brought forward the decree."

Do any of you see that by the passage of this decree the City disgraced herself, or laid herself open to the sneers or ridicule which this man says will be levelled at her if I am now crowned? And yet when the matter was recent and understood by every one, had it been well done it would have met with thanks; had it been ill done it would have received censure. At that time, at least, I appear to have received commendation, not dispraise or dishonor.

The time in which these things took place, I call all to witness, was at least a period when I was acknowledged to have been doing everything in the City's interest: a period in which I was in the ascendency in your councils both in speech and action, and when, by my decrees being carried into effect, honors and crowns were in consequence voted to the City and to me, and to all of you, and sacrifices and solemn processions were made by you to the Gods on account of our successes.

Philip being thus driven out of Eubœa by your arms, and by my policy and my decrees,—this I will say, though some of you should burst at hearing it,— he sought to engineer a new device against the City. Knowing that you consumed more foreign corn than all the rest of the world, he resolved to make himself master of the carrying trade, and for this purpose he came to Thrace and endeavored to incite his allies, the Byzantines, to make war against you. When they refused, saying, and saying truly, that their alliance was not for any such purpose, Philip turned round, drew a line of circumvallation about their city, and, planting his engines down, commenced its siege. I need hardly ask what was your duty in this conjuncture: it was clear to all. Who was it, however, who brought relief to the Byzantines and saved them? Who was it who then prevented the Helles- pont from passing under the control of another? It was you, Athenians; and when I say you I mean the City. And who was it that was speaking, and decree- ing, and acting in the City's behalf, giving himself up to her entirely and without reserve? It was I.—The great things which were then done in aid of all, you

cannot learn from words alone,—from the work itself
you have approved them.   That war, apart from the
glory which it conferred, brought to you a more abundant supply of all the necessaries of life at cheaper
rates than this present peace made against the City's
interests, which Æschines and his friends,—excellent
men!—with their hopes for the future, have guarded
so zealously, hopes which I trust they may be disappointed in!   Let them partake with you of the good
which you are asking of the Gods, but let there not
be meted out to you any of the things which they
have been desiring!   Read here to them the crowns
which the Byzantines and Perinthians voted to the
City in consequence of its services.

DECREE OF THE BYZANTINES.

"In the presbytership of Bosporichus, Damagetus moved in
the Assembly, with the consent of the Council, as follows:
Whereas the Athenian people has in the past displayed its good-
will to the Byzantines and to their allies and relatives the Perinthians, and has frequently sent them great assistance; and
whereas when Philip of Macedon was recently invading the
land, threatening to destroy their cities, firing the country, and
cutting down the plantations, the Athenians sent to their relief
one hundred and twenty ships, provisions, arms, and troops, and
saved them from their great peril, preserving for them their
form of government, their laws, and their tombs, it is ordered
that there be conferred by the Byzantines and Perinthians upon
the Athenians the rights of intermarriage, citizenship, property,
and domicile, the first seats at the public games, the privilege of
entering first in the Senate and Assembly after the sacrifices,

and to those who wish to reside in their cities the right to do so exempted from public burthens. Moreover, three statues, sixteen cubits in height, shall be erected upon the Bosphorus, representing the people of Athens crowned by the people of Byzantium and Perinthus, and deputations shall be sent to the public meetings of the Greeks at the Isthmian, Nemean, Olympian, and Pythian games, where proclamation shall be made of the crowns decreed by us to the Athenians, that the assembled Greeks may be certified of the virtue of the Athenians, and of the gratitude of the Byzantines and Perinthians."

Read now the decree of the people of Chersonnesus voting crowns to the Athenians.

DECREE OF THE CHERSONNESIANS.

" The people of Chersonnesus, inhabiting Sestos, Eleus, Madytus, and Alopeconesus, crown the council and people of Athens with a golden crown, of the value of sixty talents; and they will furthermore erect an altar to Gratitude and to the Athenian people, as having conferred upon them the greatest possible good, in rescuing them from Philip, and preserving to them their country, their laws, their liberties, and their temples. Thus, in all time to come, their gratitude and their desire to do every good in their power to the Athenians shall not fail. Decreed in general assembly."

Thus, not only were Chersonnesus and Byzantium saved, and the Hellespont kept from Philip's control; not only was the City honored by what my measures and my policy had effected, but to the whole world were exhibited her magnanimity and Philip's baseness. What more disgraceful and scandalous spec-

tacle than that their friend and ally should be
besieging the Byzantines? Whilst you, who had
just reason to blame them for the many acts of un-
friendliness they had formerly committed against
you, were now seen not only bearing no malice
against them; not only passing over their wrongful
conduct, but actually coming forward as their pre-
servers. For this, honor, glory, renown, were lav-
ished upon you from every side. We all know that
many public men had theretofore been crowned by
you; but when could it be shewn before my day that
the City itself had received a crown through one of
its counsellors and orators?

As to the abuse which Æschines has been pouring
out against the Eubœans and Byzantines, while he
has been reminding you of every unfriendly act they
ever perpetrated against you, I shall shew it to be
malicious and false, as I suppose you yourselves are
already satisfied. Had it been true, it was necessary
for us I should have acted in the matter as I did. In
proof of this I wish to present one or two instances
of noble acts performed by you, and this very briefly.
And we must recollect, that as with the individual in
private life, so must the City in its public career
always strive to make its future conduct emulate the
glories of the past. When the Lacedemonians were
all-powerful by sea and land, and had surrounded
Attica with their governors and garrisons, having
taken Eubœa, Tanagra, all Bœotia, Megara, Egina,

12

Cleonæ, and the other islands, you, Athenians, although the City was destitute both of ships and walls, did not hesitate to march to the aid of Haliartus, and again, a few days later, to Corinth. You might then have recalled the many grievances you had to complain of both from the Corinthians and the Thebans for their conduct in the Dekelian war. But you did not,—far from it. Nor on either of these occasions did you act from gratitude, or from ignorance of the peril. But it did not, Æschines, make the Athenians abandon those who implored them for assistance. From a sense of honor, from a love of glory, they encountered the emergency, acting wisely as well as magnanimously. For as death is the limit of life to every one, let him hide himself where he may in some obscure hole, it becomes all gallant men to strive for what is noble, holding up high hope before them, but resolved to bear firmly whatever the Gods shall award to them.

Such was your ancestors' course, such the course of the elder amongst yourselves. For when the Thebans in the height of their power after Leuctra undertook to destroy the Lacedemonians, who had never been either friendly or even well-disposed to you, but on the contrary had inflicted many and great wrongs upon your City, you prevented it. You were neither deterred by the dread of the power or reputation of the Thebans; nor did you stop to think what the men for whom you were incurring danger had formerly done against you. You thus shewed all Greece that if any people had offended you you reserved your anger for another time, but did not recall and dwell upon it when danger menaced their safety or their freedom.

Nor were these the only instances of such behavior on your part. When the Thebans recently attempted to get possession of Euboea, you would not permit it, but, forgetting the injuries of Themison and Theodorus in regard to Oropus, you succored even these very men. This was at the time we had voluntary trierarchs, of whom I was one; but it is not necessary to speak now of this.

You did well in saving the island; but you did far better in honorably restoring to those who had offended you their cities and their inhabitants of which you had made yourselves masters, forgetting all their injuries from the time they had reposed their trust in you. I omit to mention a thousand other like instances, engagements by sea and by land, expeditions of all kinds, undertaken long ago by our fathers, recently by yourselves, all for the safety and the liberties of the other Greeks.

And I who had seen the City willing to exert herself on all these occasions for the safety of others, what kind of advice did it become me to offer to her when it concerned herself? To cherish enmity against those who desired to be saved by her, and to seek for pretexts by which we might have betrayed the com-

mon cause? Just heaven! Who would not have
rightly put me to death, had I attempted even by
speech thus to tarnish the glories which belonged to
the City? I knew well that you could not of yourselves have committed a dishonorable action. Had
you desired to do so, who was there to hinder you?
Was it not in your power? And were not these evil
counsellors always present?

02~ I will now return to the next in order of my public
acts. And I desire you to look closely whether I
acted therein for the State's best interests. I saw,
Athenians, that your navy was deteriorating; the
rich were exempt from all but paltry contributions towards its support, while by the assessments upon them
the owners of moderate properties and the poorer
classes were almost stripped of their estates, and yet
the City was going behindhand. I therefore had a
law passed by which the wealthy were compelled to
contribute equitably and the poor were relieved from
oppression, the City being greatly the gainer by the
work being done in good season. Being impeached-
for this, I appealed to you, and the prosecutor did
not receive the fifth part of the votes. What sum of
money do you imagine the heads of the Symmories,
and those next to them, and even third in order,
offered to me, rather than have this law passed, or to
get it withdrawn when the prosecution against me
began? It was so large that I dare hardly name it
to you. And yet they acted prudently in doing so.

For by the old law sixteen of them being chargeable together, the contribution of each single one was little or nothing, the poorer citizens being ground to powder. By my law each citizen was rated according to his property, and he who had been formerly a contributory of only a sixteenth was now the trierarch of even two ships. For they had even ceased to be called trierarchs, but styled themselves contributories. So that to get rid of these burthens, and to escape their just liabilities, there is nothing they would not have given. Read now, first, the decree under which I was prosecuted, and then the operative parts of the old law, and the one proposed by me.

DECREE.

"In the archonship of Polycles, on the sixteenth day of Boedromion, during the presidency of the tribe Hippothoontis, Demosthenes, son of Demosthenes the Pæanian, proposed a law in regard to trierarchs, in place of the old law of contributories to trierarchs. It was passed by the Council and people, whereupon Patrocles of Phlyus impeached Demosthenes, but not receiving the requisite number of votes, he has paid the fine of five hundred drachmas."

Read now the honest schedule of the old law !

SCHEDULE.

"The trierarchs shall be appointed sixteen to each trireme from the contributories in the Companies, from twenty-five years of age up to forty, each contributing equally to the expense."

Read now the enacting part of my law.

SCHEDULE.

"Trierarchs shall be chosen for a trireme according to the valuation of their property, the rate being fixed at ten talents. Should properties be valued in excess of this sum, let the charge go up as high as three ships and a tender, according to assessment. In the same ratio let those whose properties are assessed below ten talents contribute together until that sum is reached."

Do I seem, then, Athenians, to have assisted the poorer classes in a slight degree, or would the rich have given a small amount of money to have escaped their just burthen? I have a right, therefore, to claim credit not only for not having yielded in this matter, and for having escaped the impeachment, but for having introduced a profitable law which was found by experience to suit the work in hand. During the whole war our naval expeditions were fitted out under this law of mine, and not only no trierarch sought exemption from it of you as unjust, or took refuge from it in Munychia, or was imprisoned by the superintendents of marine, but no ship was ever abandoned at sea to the City's loss, nor was any left in port from inability to get away, all of which had often occurred under the old law. And the reason was that the tax pressed too heavily upon those who were unable to bear it, and impossibilities could not be achieved.

I transferred the trierarchies from the poor to the rich, and all that was wanted was at once found done. And not only do I deserve credit because I laid down a line of policy from which honor, and reputation, and power accrued to the City, but no single measure of mine was mean, or rigorous, or base, or hard, or unworthy of the State. This was my plain course not only in matters regarding the City, but in what affected Greece generally. In our own affairs I did not set the favor of the wealthy above the City's interests; nor in the affairs of Greece did I prefer Philip's gifts and allurements to the common advantage of all the Greeks. ——

It remains for me to speak about the proclamation and my accounting, for I think it sufficiently clear, from what I have said, that I have always done the best for you, and that I have been throughout well-disposed and zealous in your service. I shall, therefore, pass over my most important public acts, first, because it is proper that I should now speak upon the question of illegality; next, should I say nothing further about them, your own consciousness of them shall equally avail me.

As to most of Æschines's muddled statements about the laws contradicting the decree in my behalf, I think, by heavens, that neither you could understand what he said, nor I, I am sure, follow them at all. I will give you, however, a plain rule by which to try this question. I am so far from saying the contrary, as he has just been slanderously charging me with, that I now admit I shall hold myself accountable all my life for whatever I have taken in hand and managed for you. But for what I have given from my own private fortune to the people, I say,—do you hear, Æschines?—I have never been accountable for a single day: nor would any one else be, were he even one of the nine archons. Where can be found the law so stuffed with harshness and injustice as first to rob of thanks the man who in giving out of his private means performs a beneficent and liberal act, and then turn him over to an account before malignants of what he has thus given? There cannot be. If he says there is, let him shew it; I shall be satisfied and hold my peace. There never was such a law, Athenians; but this libeller says, because I was administering the Theoric fund at the time I so gave, "the Council has honored him while he was still accountable." Oh Calumniator, it was not for anything for which I was accountable, but in regard to my free-will offerings! But again, he says, "you were a commissioner for repairing the walls." And for this very thing I was rightly commended; for I gave what was expended upon them, without reckoning with the public. A reckoning requires the exhibition of accounts and their settlement; but a free gift merits thanks and commendation. And it was for this that Ctesiphon brought forward his decree; from an hundred instances I shall shew that this has been so settled, not only by your laws, but by your equitable practice.

First, Nausicles, the general, was many times

crowned by you for what he gave to the public out of his own property. So when Diotimus gave shields, and again Charidemus, they were both crowned.

So, also, Neoptolemus, here present, who was superintendent of many public works, was frequently honored for what he gave towards them. Hard indeed would it be were it not permitted to one exercising a public employment to give of his own means to the City towards the work in hand, or to be compelled to render an account of it instead of receiving thanks for his liberality. To prove the correctness of my assertions, take the decrees passed in regard to these citizens, and read them.

DECREE.

"In the archonship of Demonicus of Phlyus, on the twenty-sixth day of Boedromion, by the advice of the Council and People, Callias of Phrearrii moved as follows: The Council and People think it proper that Nausicles, the general of arms, be crowned, because when two thousand Athenian heavy-armed troops were in Imbros to assist the Athenian colonists in that island, and Philo charged with the supplies was prevented by stormy weather from sailing thither and paying them, Nausicles relieved them out of his own funds without making any reclamation upon the City: proclamation of the coronation to be made at the Dionysiac festivals at the representation of the new tragedies."

ANOTHER DECREE.

"The Senators declaring it to be by the advice of the Council, Callias of Phrearrii moved as follows: Whereas Charidemus, commander of the heavy-armed troops when in Salamis, and Diotimus, commander of the cavalry, certain of our troops having been despoiled of their arms by the enemy in the engagement by the river, supplied the young soldiery out of their own private means with shields to the number of eight hundred, it is decreed by the Council and people that Charidemus and Diotimus shall be crowned with golden crowns, proclamation of the coronation to be made at the great Panathenaic festivals during the gymnastic games, and at the Dionysiac festivals during the representation of the new tragedies. The junior archons, the Senators, and the Masters of the Games will take charge of the proclamation."

Each of these citizens, while accountable in regard to the employments which he exercised, was not so as to the matters for which he was crowned. Nor I either.—For what was just and proper in their case is surely equally so in mine. I gave;—I was commended for this;—nor was I to be accountable for what I had thus given.—I exercised a public charge; —I rendered my accounts of this;—not of what I gave. But by Jove, say you, I exercised my charge unfairly.—Why then, I ask, did you not, as you were present when the auditors passed my accounts, object to them?

But that you may see that he himself testifies for me that I was crowned for what I was not accountable for, look at the whole decree which was written in my behalf, and from what he has not attacked in it his malignity will be evident in what he has attacked. Read it.

DECREE.

"In the archonship of Euthycles, on the twenty-second day of the month Pyanepsion, in the presidency of the tribe Œneis, Ctesiphon, son of Leosthenes the Anaphlystian, moved as follows: Whereas Demosthenes, son of Demosthenes the Pæanian, whilst he was superintendent of the repair of the walls, gave to the people three talents of his own money towards the prosecution of the work, and also whilst he was administrator of the Theoric fund gave to the sacred envoys for their sacrifices one hundred minæ, it is decreed by the Council and people of Athens that the said Demosthenes, son of Demosthenes the Pæanian, be commended for the public spirit and good feeling ever manifested by him to the Athenian people, and that he be crowned with a golden crown, the coronation to be proclaimed in the Theatre at the Dionysiac festivals during the representation of the new tragedies. The Masters of the Games will see to the proclamation."

It was not, then, for anything which I gave· that you attacked the decree: it is for what the Council resolved should be done to me for what I gave that you arraigned it. The receiving of the gifts from me he therefore admits to be within the law;—it is the conferring of thanks for the gifts which he accuses as against the law. Where, in the name of heaven, could there be found a more thoroughly depraved and wicked man the enemy of the Gods, if it be not he?

As to the proclamation in regard to the crowning in the Theatre, I pass it by, as it has been done to thousands of persons thousands of times, I myself having been often crowned there. But you are so stupid and senseless, Æschines, that, by the Gods, you are not able to perceive that while the crown confers the same honor upon the recipient, let the coronation take place where it may, it is in favor of those who decree it that proclamation of it is ordered to be made in the Theatre. For when the whole people hear this they are stimulated to do good service to the State, in their admiration of the kindness of those conferring the honor rather than of him upon whom it is conferred. Wherefore it was that the City long since enacted this law. Take it now and read it.

· LAW.

"Whenever persons shall be crowned by the different demes, proclamation shall be made of the fact in each deme, unless the whole community or the Council shall decree the crown. In such cases the proclamation may be made in the Theatre, at the Dionysiac festivals."

Do you hear, Æschines, the law speaks clearly, "unless the whole community or the Council shall decree the crown, in such cases proclamation may be made in the Theatre, at the Dionysiac festivals." Why, then, O miserable man, do you prevaricate? Why do you weave idle tales? Why do you not, after this, take a dose of hellebore? Is it not scandalous, that undertaking a prosecution out of hatred, and not for any illegality, you should pervert some laws, and take scraps from others which it was essential should be presented entire to those who are sworn to decide according to the laws? And you who are asking this are speaking, forsooth, of what becomes a friend of the people; just as if, after having ordered a statue according to a given pattern, you take care that the contractor shall never be able to conform to his agreement: or as if the true friend of the people is to be ascertained by words only, and not by actions and public conduct. And you bawl out, as if from a cart, your filthy vituperations such as may suit you and your breeding, but in no wise fit for me to speak.

Men of Athens, there is this difference, I think, between defamation and a legal charge :—the charge refers to illegal acts to which the laws assign their proper punishment; — defamation is sustained by mere invective, with which enemies, according to their nature, bespatter each other. Our ancestors, indeed, built these Courts of justice, I assume, not that you might be brought into them from your private business to listen to the abuse which men heap upon each other in personal wrangles, but that we might convict in them those who have committed illegal acts against the State. Æschines, knowing this fully as well as I, has nevertheless chosen to vituperate, instead of to present an accusation. It is not right, therefore, that he should withdraw without getting the worst of it.—But I will come to this point again;—I now desire to ask him this question.

Should any one ask you, Æschines, whether you

are the City's enemy or mine, you would doubtless answer, mine. Yet you failed to proceed against me according to law for these things, as a criminal, at the time of the audits of my accounts, during the prosecutions against me, and in other ways. After I have been entirely absolved by the laws, by lapse of time, by prescription, by being oftentimes tried, but never adjudged guilty, you are now opposing me as to measures which there is a necessity of the City more or less sharing the credit of, since they concerned the public:—See, then, whether you are not the enemy of your countrymen, while you are pretending to be only mine.

Since, then, the proper and just mode of deciding has been pointed out to you all, it is right, it seems, although I am by nature unaccustomed to use abusive language, that in consequence of the slanders—many and false—spoken by him, I should mention a few absolutely necessary particulars about him, and shew you who this fellow is, and what are his belongings, who undertakes thus recklessly to defame, who finds fault with my words, and who has been pouring out abuse that any moderate person would hesitate even to mention. If, indeed, my accuser were Æacus, Rhadamanthus, or Minos, instead of a babbling hack of the market-place, a pestiferous scribe, I am sure he never would so have spoken, nor would he so load down his discourse (bawling out as in a play) with such phrases as " O earth, O sun, O virtue," and the like. Nor would he appeal to conscience and education, by which good is distinguished from evil.—These things, I presume, you all heard him speaking of. Scum of the earfh, what part have you or yours with virtue? Or what knowledge have you of what is honorable or its opposite? Whence could you get it? How could you esteem it? What justice is there in your talking about education, of which if one were truly possessed he would never talk about it himself, and would even blush should another speak of it before him? Those who are destitute of it, as you are, when they stupidly lay claim to it only cause disgust in their hearers when they so speak, in no other wise succeeding.

I am not at a loss what to say about you and yours; I am only at a loss what to say first. Shall I tell how your father, Tromes, was the slave of Elpias, the schoolmaster, hard by the temple of Theseus, and how he wore heavy shackles on his feet and a yoke about his neck? Or how your mother made use of her morning nuptials in the stews with her hero, the Calamite, to rear up her fair statuesque son, the great third-rate actor? Or how Phormio, the galley flute-player, Dion the Phrearrian's slave, took her out of this fine way of living? But, by the Gods, I pause, not lest I should say what is not befitting him, but lest I should seem to speak of things unbecoming myself. I shall, therefore, quit this subject, and start from the life which he has lived himself.

In all this there is nothing which the people has not execrated. Was it not lately—lately, do I say?—in fact, only yesterday—he became an Athenian and an orator; and, adding two syllables to his father's name, made Atrometus out of Tromes? His mother he called very splendidly Glaucothea, whom every one knew before as Empusa, because of her doing and submitting to everything, as her surname plainly shewed. How otherwise could she have got it?

But how thankless and of how depraved a nature you are!—When, by the favor of the Athenians, you are made a freeman and rich, from a slave and a pauper, you return no thanks for this, but hire yourself out to work against them.—As to anything which is in doubt whether he spoke in behalf of the City, I say nothing. I shall only bring to your recollection what he has been openly proved to have done for our enemies.

Who amongst you does not recollect the outlawed Antiphon, who entered the City under a commission from Philip to set fire to your ship-yards? When I took him from his hiding-place in Piræus, and brought him before the Assembly, this malignant fellow bawled out to you that I was committing an outrage in a free community, that I was insulting the unfortunate, that I was entering a house without a warrant,—and he had him discharged. Had not the Council of the Areopagus, observing how from incaution you had fallen into error, taken hold of the matter, and sought him out and brought him before you again, the miscreant would have been rescued and escaped the hands of justice, spirited away by this solemn prater. But you put him to the torture, and despatched him, as you should this Æschines.

When you subsequently, from the same inconsiderateness, nominated him as your advocate in the affair of the Temple at Delos,—an inconsiderateness with which you have proceeded to your disadvantage in many matters of importance,—the Council of the Areopagus, to whom you had referred the matter for determination, taking cognizance of what he had done in the case just spoken of, at once set him aside as a traitor, and substituted Hyperides in his place. And this they did taking their votes from the altar itself, not a single one being cast in favor of this wretch. And to shew you I speak truly, call me now the witnesses.

WITNESSES.

"Upon the demand of Demosthenes, on behalf of all their colleagues Callias of Sunium, Zeno of Phlyus, Cleon of Phalerum, and Demonicus of Marathon, declare that the people having elected Æschines to be their advocate to the Amphictyons, in the matter of the Temple of Delos, they adjudged Hyperides to be more worthy to represent the City :—and Hyperides was sent."

Thus, therefore, after he had been chosen, the Council removed him, and preferred another, assert-

13

ing him to be a traitor and inimical to your interests. This, then, is one of this fine young man's political acts, like what he has been charging me with, is not it? Let me call to your notice another one.

When Philip sent Python, the Byzantine, to us, and with him the ambassadors of all his allies, that he might bring discredit upon the City by denouncing her injustice, I yielded not to nor recoiled from Python's insolence and his stream of abuse against you;—I withstood him to the face and answered him back. So far from abandoning the righteous cause of the City, I exposed Philip's injustice, so that even his allies rose up and admitted it. This man, however, stood by assisting him, and bearing false testimony against his country.

This is not all. Again, some time afterwards, he was detected going into Thraso's house, with Anaxinus the spy. Now, he who is found consulting in secret with an emissary of the enemy, is himself a spy in heart, and an enemy of his country. Call me here the witnesses to establish the truth of my assertion.

WITNESSES.

"Keledemus, son of Cleon; Hyperides, son of Callæschrus; Nicomachus, son of Diophantes, testify for Demosthenes as they swore in the presence of the generals, that they saw Æschines, son of Atrometus, the Cothocidian, entering the house of Thraso by night, and conferring with Anaxinus, who had been adjudged to be a spy of Philip's. This testimony was given before Nikias on the third of the month Hecatombeon."

I omit a thousand other acts of the same kind, and for this reason. I could point to many more cases from which this man, during the whole of this time, could be shewn to have been assisting your enemies, whilst he was vilifying me. But these things are neither very accurately remembered by you, nor do they beget in you any resentment. By a certain vicious habit, you give ample license to any one who wishes to trip up and defame him who is counselling in your behalf, thus trading against the interests of the City the pleasure and satisfaction you derive from listening to attacks upon character. It is, therefore, always safer and easier to serve your enemies for pay against you, than to urge a line of policy by which your interests may be advanced.

If, however, before the war broke out it was scandalous for Æschines to act publicly with Philip against his country,—heavens and earth, why should it not have been!—Pass this by, however.—But after our ships had been openly seized, the Chersonnesus ravaged, and Philip himself was advancing towards Attica, nothing being longer in doubt, and war flagrant, what then did this miserable mouther of iambics do in your behalf? You can find no decree proposed by Æschines, great or small, for the advantage of the City. If he says there is, let him shew it now,—I yield him my time for the purpose. But there is nothing of the kind. Of two things, therefore, one is clear; either he had nothing to propose

better than what I advised; or, seeking the advantage
of our enemies, he did not advise upon the subject.
But although he wrote no decrees, he was not at
all silent whenever any mischief was to be worked
against you:—then it was impossible for any one
else to speak.

The City, it seemed, was able to bear up to this
time what he had been secretly contriving against it.
But what he now did, men of Athens, put the finish-
ing stroke to all his former misdeeds;—the matter
about which he spent such a waste of words, passing
in review the decrees concerning the Locrians of
Amphissa, when he was endeavoring to twist the
truth. But this cannot be:—far from it. Never can
you wash yourself clean of what was then done by
you. You shall speak your words in vain.

In your presence, men of Athens, I invoke the
Gods and Goddesses who hold Attica under their
fostering care; above all, the Pythian Apollo, your
patron; and I pray them all, as I shall speak truth to
you,—and I spoke it out instantly before the people
when the matter was first broached by this miscreant,
(I knew it, I knew it well on the instant,)—as I
speak truth, so may they grant me their protection
and my salvation! But if from private hatred or
enmity I falsely accuse this man, may they forever
deprive me of all that is good!

Why do I make these imprecations, and why am I
thus vehemently excited? It is because although I

have the proofs lying in your archives, from which
to establish my assertions; although you yourselves
must clearly remember the facts, I fear lest you will
never believe this man to have been wicked enough
to perpetrate such a crime,—as happened before,
when he brought about the ruin of the Phocians by
making use of false testimony against them to you.
This, this is the man who first lighted up the war in
Amphissa which made Philip the leader of the Amphictyons, which brought him to Elatea, and which
finally overturned the affairs of Greece; this is the
man who contrived and plotted all,—the cause of all
your ruin!

When I arose in the Assembly, and protested and
cried out, "You are bringing the war into Attica,
Æschines, an Amphictyonic war," those who were
ranged on his side would not suffer me to speak; the
others sat by astonished, and persuaded themselves
that I was making an empty charge against him from
private enmity. But, men of Athens, although you
were then prevented, hear to-day what was the real
origin of this business; in what way the whole thing
was contrived; how it was finally completed. You
shall see that the thing was well concocted; you shall
be greatly assisted in understanding the history of
the times; and you shall comprehend how great was
the ability of Philip.

There was neither end nor deliverance for Philip
from the war with you, unless he could make the The-

bans and Thessalians your enemies. For although
your generals fought against him both unskilfully
and unsuccessfully, still, from the war itself and from
the cruisers at sea he suffered greatly. He could
neither export from his own country what was raised
in it, nor could he import into it what was necessary
for him, as he was not only inferior to you by sea,
but he was unable to penetrate Attica unless the
Thessalians followed him and the Thebans gave him
a free passage through their country. It thus happened to him, that although he overcame your generals—such as they were—(I pass over this, however,) from the very nature of the situation and
from your relative positions, he was at a great disadvantage. Should he, however, by reason of his
own private quarrel, try to persuade the Thessalians
or Thebans to march against you, he thought he
could never induce them to do so; but if by the pretext of a common cause he could succeed in being
chosen general, he readily hoped he might either
cheat or persuade them to aid his views. What then
should he put his hand to? You shall see how well.
he contrived.—He would create an Amphictyonic
war, and introduce trouble into the Assembly at
Thermopylæ, and then they would at once think him
necessary to them. Should any of the presbyters,
however, sent either by him or his allies, agitate
the subject, he knew it would be looked upon with
suspicion by the Thebans and Thessalians, and that

every one would be thus put upon his guard. But if he could bring about that the presbyter should be an Athenian, sent by you his opponents, the matter would easily escape notice. And so it turned out.

How, then, did he work this? HE PURCHASED ÆS-CHINES.) No one, as I suppose, either foreseeing or suspecting the thing, (you know how these matters are generally done by you,) Æschines was nominated as deputy, and chosen by a shew of three or four hands.

Clothed with this honor from the City, he came to the Amphictyonic Council, and disregarding everything else, hastened to accomplish the purpose for which he was hired. Putting together specious and false statements as to the origin of the dedication of the Kirrhæan plain, as he had to deal only with the presbyters who were simple and unsuspecting, he persuaded them to resolve upon a perambulation of the district which the Amphissians declared they were cultivating as their own, but which he pronounced to be within the sacred precincts. The Locrians had then no controversy with us, as he has falsely asserted here to-day. You may know the truth from this. It was impossible, I suppose, for the Locrians to have had a controversy with us, without first sending us a citation. Who ever summoned you? In whose archonship was it done? Name him, if he is known—shew it. You cannot. This hollow artifice you made use of, and you falsified.

Whilst the Amphictyons were perambulating the plain, in pursuance of Æschines's advice, the Locrians fell upon them and almost destroyed them all, even carrying off some of the presbyters. Accusations following, and hostilities being in consequence imminent, Cottyphus was at first appointed to lead an army composed of Amphictyons against the Amphissians. But as some of the troops did not come at all, and as those that came did nothing, the traitors among the Thessalians, and in the other cities, who were on the lookout, forthwith urged the choice of Philip as general at the approaching Council : and they made use of specious arguments. For they said, they must either raise a subsidy for the support of an army of mercenaries and fine those who did not contribute, or select Philip. Why waste words about this ? Philip was chosen general; and immediately drawing his forces together, and advancing as if against Kirrha, he bade good-bye forever to the Kirrhæans and Locrians, and forthwith took possession of Elatea.

If the Thebans upon witnessing this had not at once changed their minds, and taken sides with you, the whole thing would have burst upon our City like a mountain torrent. Now, indeed, for the moment they stopped him ;—chiefly, men of Athens, through the kindness of some divinity to you, next, as much as lay in the power of one man, through me.

Give me the decrees, and the dates in which everything took place, that you may see how one infamous head has brought about, unpunished, these great misfortunes.   Read the decrees.

DECREE.

"In the priesthood of Clinagoras at the Spring Council, it was resolved by the deputies and councillors of the Amphictyons, as well as by the General Assembly, that whereas the Amphissians have entered upon the sacred district, sowing grain thereupon, and dividing it up for pasturage, the deputies and councillors are directed to mark its boundaries by proper monuments, and to forbid the Amphissians from trespassing for the future."

ANOTHER DECREE.

"In the priesthood of Clinagoras, at the Spring Sessions, it was resolved by the deputies and councillors of the Amphictyons, and by the General Assembly, that whereas the Amphissians have entered upon the sacred plain, and have ploughed it and divided it up for pasturage, and when forbidden to proceed have assembled in arms and resisted the General Assembly of the Greeks with violence, and wounded some of their number, it is now ordered that Cottyphus, the Arcadian chosen as General of the Amphictyons, be despatched to Philip of Macedon to request him to come to the aid of Apollo and the Amphictyons, and not to suffer the God to be insulted by the impious Amphissians; and that therefore the Greeks assembled in the Amphictyonic Council have elected him as their General with absolute powers."

Read me now the dates at which these things took place : they happened whilst Æschines was an Amphictyonic deputy.   Read.—

DATES.

"Mnesitheides being Archon, on the sixteenth day of the month Anthesterion."

Give me now the letter which, as the Thebans did not respond to him, Philip sent to his allies in Peloponnesus. You may see clearly from it he was concealing the true aspect of the measures he was adopting against Greece and the Thebans and yourselves, whilst he was pretending to act for the common interest under the orders of the Amphictyons. These pretexts and these shams this man furnished him with. Read.—

PHILIP'S LETTER.

"Philip, King of the Macedonians, to the Magistrates and Councillors of the Peloponnesian allies, and to the other allies, Greeting. Whereas the Locrians called Ozolian dwelling in Amphissa have profaned the temple of Apollo at Delphi, and with arms in their hands have violated the sacred plain, now, with your assistance, I desire to avenge the God, and to punish the men who have committed these sacrilegious acts. We ask you, therefore, to assemble with arms in Phocis, supplied with provisions for forty days, in the coming month of Loos, as we style it, called Boedromion by the Athenians, and Panemus by the Corinthians. Those who shall so assemble in mass with us we shall treat as friends, and those not joining us as enemies."

See how he avoids speaking of his private ends, and skulks behind Amphictyonic reasons. Who sup-

plied him with these pretexts? Who prepared them
for him? Who has been the head and front of all
the evils which have thus been wrought? Is it not
this man? Do not go about, Athenians, saying that
Greece has suffered all her woes from ONE MAN.
Heavens and earth! It has not been from one man,
but from many wretches found in every city. And
Æschines is one of them; whom, were I bound to
speak nothing but the literal truth, I should not hesitate to denounce as a common pest, the cause of all
the destruction of men, places, and cities, that afterwards took place. The sower of the seed is the
author of the crop of ruin which springs up. How
you can look upon him without at once turning
away, I wonder; but there is a veil, it seems to me,
between you and the truth.

It has happened to me, in handling the various acts
done by this man against his country, to touch upon
matters which I myself proposed in opposition to
him. For many reasons, Athenians, I desire you to
hear me upon them; but chiefly because it would
be disgraceful in you not to be willing to listen to
the account of that which I spent so much labor in
accomplishing.

Seeing then that the Thebans, and you too, influ-
enced by those who were doing Philip's work—the
corrupt men in each city—were overlooking and not
providing for what was dangerous and to be guarded
against by you, namely, suffering Philip's strength to

increase whilst you were hating and quarrelling with each other, I was ever on the lookout to prevent this being accomplished. Nor did I thus act from my own opinion alone; for I well knew that Aristophon and Eubulus, who differed greatly as to other matters, had ever desired to bring about this friendly feeling,—being always of one mind upon this point. Those men, vile wretch, whom you fawned upon when living, you are not now ashamed to attack when dead! For in inveighing against me about the Theban alliance, you bring a much graver accusation against them, since they advised the measure long before I did.

But I must go back now.—When Æschines had got up the Amphissian war, and whilst others, uniting with him here, were working up this enmity against Thebes, Philip was marching against you; this was the purpose for which these men had embroiled the two cities. And if we had not bestirred ourselves a little we should not have been able. to recover, so far forward had they brought the matter. In what position you stood to each other you shall learn from these decrees and answers.

Read now the decrees.

DECREE.

"In the archonship of Heropythus, on the twenty-fifth day of the month Elaphebolion, in the presidency of the Erectheian tribe, it was resolved, by the advice of the Council and Generals, as follows: Whereas Philip has taken possession of certain cities of our neighbors, and is besieging others; but, above all, is preparing to march against Attica, disregarding our treaties, and intending to break his oath and the peace, and to overturn our common engagements, therefore it is resolved by the Council and the people to send ambassadors to Philip, who shall confer with him, and endeavor to persuade him, above all, to keep faithfully his agreements and treaties with us ; or if not, at least to give sufficient time to the City to deliberate, and to grant an armistice until the month Thargelion. There have been chosen as deputies from the Council, Simus of Anagyrus, Euthydemus of Phlyus, Bulagoras of Alopeke."

ANOTHER DECREE.

"In the archonship of Heropythus, on the last day of the month Munychion, it was resolved, by the advice of the Polemarch : Whereas Philip is endeavoring to bring the Thebans into hostilities with us, and is preparing to take possession, with all his forces, of the places bordering upon Attica, disregarding the existing treaties between us, it is resolved by the Council and people to send a herald and envoys unto him to endeavor to persuade him to grant an armistice, that the people may have an opportunity to consider the matter, for the people has not now determined to march out in the event of anything reasonable. Were chosen as envoys from the Council, Nearchus, son of Sosinomus ; Polycrates, son of Epiphron; and as herald from the people, Eunomus, the Anaphlystian."

Read now Philip's answers.

ANSWER TO THE ATHENIANS.

"Philip, King of Macedon, to the Council and people of Athens, Greeting.

"I am not ignorant of the design which you have had from the beginning, and which you vehemently desire to carry out, of

gaining over the Thessalians and Thebans, as well as the Bœotians. They, however, have thought better of this matter, and
do not wish to adopt your views, but to stand by their own interest. You now turn round and send a herald and envoys to
remind us of our treaties, and to ask for an armistice, although
you have been in no wise wronged by us. I have listened, however, to your envoys, and am ready to accede to your demand
and grant the armistice, if you will dismiss your evil counsellors, and disgrace them as they deserve. Farewell."

ANSWER TO THE THEBANS.

"Philip, King of Macedon, to the Council and people of
Thebes, Greeting. I have received your letter, in which you
renew concord and peace with me. But I understand that the
Athenians have been using efforts to induce you to join them in
carrying out their plans. At first I blamed you for suffering
yourselves to be persuaded by their promises to follow their
advice. But knowing now that you earnestly seek to preserve
peace with me rather than to follow the opinions of others, I
rejoice and praise you on many accounts, but chiefly because in
so acting you have consulted your own safety, and preserve your
kind feelings towards me. It will, I hope, be of no small importance to you if you abide in this purpose. Farewell."

Philip, having thus by these means embroiled the
cities, puffed up by the decrees and his answers to
them, advanced with his forces against Elatea and
took possession of it, thinking that happen what
might, you and the Thebans would never be united.
Though you all know the alarm which this caused to
Athens, hear from me a few words about it, and
these only the most necessary.

It was evening.—A messenger arrived to inform the Presidents that Elatea was taken. Immediately rising from supper, some of them drove from their tents those who were engaged in traffic in the market-place, and set fire to the booths; whilst others sent for the generals, and called out the trumpeter: great was the excitement in the City. The next morning at daybreak the Presidents called the Council together in their Chamber, and you all assembled in public meeting;—before the Council had advised or offered anything for consideration, every deme was seated in its place upon the hill-side. When the Council arrived, and the Presidents proclaimed the news, and introduced the messenger who spoke out his message, the herald demanded, "Who desires to address the meeting?" No one stood forth. After the herald had many times made the same demand, no one responded, although all the generals, all the orators were present, and their country by her common voice called upon each citizen to advise concerning her safety; for when the herald lifted up his voice, according to law, it is right to call it the common voice of our country. If it behooved all who desired the salvation of their country to come forward, all of you and the rest of the Athenians would have stood up, and mounted the platform; for all, I well know, desired her salvation. Had it concerned the rich in particular, the three hundred would have risen up. Had it concerned those who were both warmly attached to their country and also wealthy, they who immediately afterwards gave largely for the common interests would have been there, for they gave from patriotism as well as wealth. But, as it appeared, the day and the occasion required not merely a rich and patriotic citizen, but one who had followed the subject from the very beginning, and could correctly understand why it was that Philip was thus acting, and what was his ulterior purpose. He who was ignorant of this, or who had not followed it carefully for a long time, was totally unfit, notwithstanding his patriotism and his wealth, either to see what it was necessary to do, or to advise you how to do it.

I was the man who appeared on that day, and who, ascending the platform, addressed you. What I then told you, you should now listen to attentively for two reasons: first, that you may know that I alone, of all the orators and counsellors, did not desert the patriot's post in that hour of danger, but both by speech and written decrees advised what was most useful to you in your time of peril; next, because by spending a little time upon this you will much more readily comprehend all the rest of the policy of the day. I spoke as follows: " Those persons, I thought, who were greatly troubled at the Thebans being under Philip's control, ignored the real state of things, for I well knew that if this had been the case we should have not only heard of Philip being in Elatea, but on our very borders. I was clearly, however, of opinion that he was coming to Thebes to bring this about.—How the matter now stands," I said, " hear from me.

" Philip has won over many of the Thebans by bribing some and deceiving others: those, however, who have withstood him from the first, and are now opposed to him, he will in no wise be able to gain. What, then, is his purpose, and why has he occupied Elatea ? By making a great shew of strength and displaying his arms he has raised up and inspired confidence in his adherents, and to the same extent depressed his enemies. He will thus compel these last either to join him through fear, which they do not wish to do, or they will be crushed out completely. If, therefore," said I, " we are now disposed to remember the old offences of the Thebans against us, and to distrust them as enemies, we shall be doing exactly what Philip wants; and I fear that even those of them who are now unfriendly will join him, and then all having Philippized with one consent, he and they will march together against Attica.

" If you will listen to me, and look dispassion- ately at what I am going to propose, I think I can shew what is best to be done, and remove the present danger from the City. What, then, do I propose ?

" First of all dispel your present apprehension, and feel and fear for the Thebans. The danger is much nearer to them than to us, for to them the peril is immediate. Next, let all who are able march at once with the cavalry to Eleusis, that every one may see you are in arms. Your partisans in Thebes will thus be enabled to speak out freely on the right side equally with their opponents, when they know that while there is a force at Elatea to back up the traitors who have sold their country to Philip, you are prepared to stand by them and assist them, should any one attack them, while they desire to contend for their country's freedom.

"Further, I recommend that ten ambassadors be chosen, with equal power with the generals, to fix the time for going thither and for the march out. When the ambassadors shall reach Thebes, how do I propose the question shall be dealt with? Give me here your earnest attention. Endeavor to obtain nothing from the Thebans, (to attempt it at such a time would be base,) but say to them we have come to aid them, if they desire it, in their time of extreme peril, as we foresee better than they what is going to happen. Should they accept our offer, and hearken to us, we shall have obtained what we wish, and our conduct will wear a color worthy of the City; should we be unsuccessful, then they will have themselves to blame for having mismanaged their business, and we shall have done nothing mean or dishonorable."

Having thus spoken, and much more to the same effect, I descended and sat down. Every one con-

curred. Not a dissenting voice was heard. I not
only spoke thus, but I wrote the decree; I not only
wrote the decree, but I went on the embassy; I not
only went on the embassy, but I persuaded the Thebans. I went through with everything from the beginning to the end, and gave myself up entirely to
you, in the existing danger to the City. Bring me
the decree which was then passed.

What name then, Æschines, do you wish me to
affix to you and what to myself upon that day? Shall.
I call *myself* Batalus, as you have done, slandering
and vilifying me; and *you* not merely a common
hero, but one from the stage, Chresphontes, or
Creon, or Œnomaus, whom you played once at Col-
lyttus, and broke down so abominably in? On that
day I, Batalus the Pæanian, seemed to be worth
much more to our country than you, Œnomaus the
Cothocidian. You, indeed, were not of the slightest
use to her; while I did everything which became the
good citizen. Read the decree:

THE DECREE OF DEMOSTHENES.

"In the archonship of Nausicles, in the presidency of the
Æantian tribe, on the sixteenth day of the month Scirophorion,
Demosthenes, son of Demosthenes of Pæania, moved as follows:
Whereas Philip, King of Macedon, has been shewn in the past
to have violated the treaties of peace made between him and the
Athenian people, and to have broken his oaths, and what is
accounted just by all the Greeks, taking possession of cities not
belonging to him, even capturing some belonging to the Athe-

nians, by whose people he has been in no wise wronged : and
whereas he is now proceeding largely by violence and cruelty,
placing garrisons in some Greek cities and destroying their independence; overthrowing others, and reducing the inhabitants
to slavery; in some of them even planting Barbarians in place
of Greeks, and giving them possession of their temples and
sepulchres; in all this not acting inconsistently with his country and his own character in thus using in excess his present
fortune, in utter oblivion of his having become unexpectedly
great by accident from a humble beginning: and whereas the
Athenian people, whilst it saw him taking cities of Barbarians
and its own, deemed it a matter of less importance that it was
wronged by him; but now that it has witnessed Grecian cities,
some insulted and others ravaged by Philip, it considers it a
great outrage, and to be unworthy of its ancestral glory to look
on and see the Greeks enslaved: Therefore, it is resolved by the
Council and people of Athens, addressing themselves and sacrificing to the Gods and tutelary heroes, under whose protection
the City and territory of the Athenians are, and laying to heart
the virtue of their forefathers, who watched over the freedom
of the Greeks with more solicitude than they did over their own
country, that they will send a fleet of two hundred ships to sea,
whose admiral shall sail up into the straits of Thermopylæ, and
their general and commander of horse shall lead our infantry
and cavalry to Eleusis; and also that ambassadors be sent to the
other Grecian cities, and first to Thebes, as Philip is nearer to
their country, to exhort them to be in no wise in dread of him,
and to hold fast to their own and the common liberties of Greece,
assuring them that the Athenian people has dismissed from her
recollection any old animosities between the two cities, and will
now assist the Thebans with her power and her means, and with
military engines and with arms, regarding it as honorable to contend with each other for the headship of their common country,
but deeming it unworthy of their glory and the virtue of their

ancestors to submit to the rule of a man of foreign race, and to abandon their leadership to him.

"Moreover, the Athenian people does not regard the people of Thebes as alien in descent or race, and bears in mind the acts of kindness shewn by their ancestors to the ancestors of the Thebans. For when the descendants of Hercules were kept out of their hereditary sovereignty by the Peloponnesians, Athens restored them to it, subduing with force of arms those who were endeavoring to resist the posterity of Hercules. We also received and succored Œdipus and his banished companions, and have rendered many other acts of kindness and good-will to the Thebans.

"Wherefore the Athenian people will not now withhold its assistance from the Thebans and the other Greeks. Let an alliance then be entered into with them, with the right of intermarriage, and let oaths be mutually given and received: Ambassadors, Demosthenes, son of Demosthenes of Pæania; Hyperides, son of Cleander of Sphettium; Mnesitheides, son of Antiphanes of Phrearrii; Democrates, son of Sophilus of Phlyus; Callæschrus, son of Diotimus of Cothocidæ."

This was the beginning and foundation of our connection with Thebes, the two Cities before this having been plunged by these men into hatred, distrust, and enmity. And this decree dispelled the danger which menaced **the** City like the morning mists. THEN was the moment for an honest politician to proclaim a better counsel than the one adopted;—and not *now* to rail at what had been done. For the statesman and the demagogue, differing in everything, are in this respect most unlike: the former states his views openly before the crisis, and makes himself responsible for them to those who give heed to him, to fortune, to the season of action, to every one;—the latter, silent when he should speak, the moment misfortune happens, is loud-tongued in abuse of all that has been done. THEN, as I said before, was the time for the upright counsellor to speak, and for wise counsels.

But I will state this extreme proposition. If even now any one can shew anything better, in whole or in part, than what I then advised, I will confess that I was wrong. If any one can to-day shew anything different, which if then done would have availed, I agree that it should not have escaped me. But if there is and was no such thing, and no one can even now suggest it, what was the true counsellor to do? Was it not to choose the best thing that presented itself?—This I then did, Æschines, when the herald proclaimed, "Who present desires to give advice,"—not, "Who wishes to quarrel with the past,"—nor, "Who wishes to forecast the future." You then sat silent in the Assembly, whilst I came forward and spoke.—But although you spoke not at that time, do it now. Tell us what measures would then have been useful;—what favorable chance was then overlooked: what alliance, what conjuncture in which I should have placed my countrymen, was omitted?

The past is taken from us all,—no one undertakes to advise about it: it is the future, it is the present which requires the exhibition of counsel. At that time

there were dangers in the future, there were dangers
actually pressing.   Scrutinize the choice of the means
I then selected, but do not carp at the result.   For the
end is, as the Master of all things decrees; but it is
the choice of a policy which displays the judgment
of the statesman.   Do not, then, regard it as my
wrong, because it chanced to Philip to succeed in the
conflict:—the issues were in God's hands, not mine.
Shew me, however, that I did not select every means
according to the best human calculation, working in
this justly, and carefully, and laboriously even beyond my strength, or that I did not propose what
was honorable and becoming and necessary to the
City; shew me this, and then find fault with me.
If the impending blow was too powerful not only
for us but for all Greece to ward off, what is it right
to do?   Is it not as if the merchant who has provided every proper equipment for his vessel, and has
done everything for its safety, when it has encountered a storm, and the rigging and tackle are broken
and shattered, should be condemned as the author of
the shipwreck?—"I was not the master of the ship,"
he might say.—"Nor was I the general, nor the
master of Fortune who herself controlled everything."

Just look at the thing and reflect for a moment.—
If, while fighting as allies of the Thebans, it befell
us as it did, what was not to have been expected, if,
instead of having them on our side, they had been
with Philip, for which end he had used every persua-

sion ? And if so great a fear and danger menaced
and overcame us when the battle was fought three
days' distance from Attica, what might not have been
expected had the disaster occurred upon our very
soil ? Do you not see that we had time to stand, to
meet together, to breathe ? Much did one day, two
days, three, enable us to do for the safety of the City.
On the other hand—but it is wrong even to speak of
what the City has been spared through the beneficence of some deity, and by the protection of this
very alliance which you have been assailing.

All that I have been saying—perhaps too much—
on this subject, is addressed to you, judges, and to
the by-standers who are listening : to this abominable
fellow, a short and plain reply shall suffice. If the
future, Æschines, was foreknown to you alone, when
the City was deliberating upon these matters, you
should then have spoken out. If you did not foresee
any more than the rest, you are as much responsible
as they. Why should you then rather accuse me as
to the result than I you ? I, indeed, was a better
citizen so far as these matters are concerned, (I refer
now to nothing else), inasmuch as I gave myself up
to what seemed to be for the general good, neither
shrinking from nor taking thought of any danger,
whilst you neither proposed anything better, (or my
measures would not have been adopted,) nor in any
wise gave your aid towards what had been agreed
upon. You were found to have acted, after the

result, as the City's worst and most malignant enemies:—while Aristratus at Naxos, and Aristolaus
at Thasos, accuse the friends of the Athenians, at
Athens Demosthenes is denounced by Æschines.
But he by whom the misfortunes of Greece are
hoarded up to build a reputation upon is himself
deserving of utter condemnation,—not to be the accuser of others; and he who profits, along with his
country's enemies, by her misfortunes, can never be
regarded as her well-wisher. You stand confest,
then, from your life and conduct, from your speech,
from your silence. Is anything to be advised for the
benefit of Athens, Æschines sits dumb. Does an
unforeseen reverse occur, Æschines is on his feet.—
Just as when disease overtakes the body, old sores
and sprains break out to worry it.

Since, however, Æschines insists so strongly upon
the result, I desire to enounce a proposition which
may at first seem paradoxical. Do not, in the name
of Jupiter and all the Gods, be astounded at it because it seems extreme, but listen without prejudice
to what I am about to say. Had the issue been
already known to you all,—had all foreseen it, and
had you, Æschines, bawled yourself hoarse in pro-
claiming it,—although you uttered not a whisper,
—even then the City should not have hesitated to
undertake what she did, having regard to her true
glory, to our ancestors, to posterity. Now indeed
she appears to have been unsuccessful, which is a

common chance when the Gods so will it. But then she would have incurred the reproach of delivering over the Greeks to Philip, if after claiming the headship of all Greece she had voluntarily descended from it. Had she then resigned without a struggle that which our forefathers spared no dangers to achieve, who would not then have spit upon you, Æschines, —not upon me, not upon the City? With what eyes, good God, could we have looked upon strangers visiting the City, had the result been what it is and Philip been chosen the lord and master of us all, the rest of our countrymen, WITHOUT US, contesting his claim? Especially when in bygone days our City had shrunk from no danger in the cause of honor, rather than repose in an inglorious security. What Greek indeed, what Barbarian does not know that the Thebans, and the Lacedemonians before them all-powerful, and the Persian king himself, would thankfully and readily have permitted Athens to take what she wished and to keep her own, had she been willing to obey the behests of the stranger and suffer him to assume the command of Greece? But such things, as it seemed to the Athenians of those days, were neither patriotic, nor natural, nor supportable; nor could any one in all past time have prevailed upon the City to succumb to the powerful evil-doer, sitting down in safe submission. No, she ever encountered every peril, in the contention for the first place, and for honor and glory. And you, your-

selves, regard this conduct as so august, and as so
conformable to your own thoughts and feelings, that
those of your ancestors who have so acted are held
by you in the highest esteem. And properly: for
who does not admire the virtue of the men who preferred to quit their city and their country, and em-
bark upon their ships, rather than endure servitude,
electing to their command Themistocles, who had so
counselled them; nay, even stoning to death Kyr-
silus, who had advised submission:—not only *him*,
but your wives also putting his wife to death. Those
Athenians sought not an orator or a general by whom
they might be enslaved; they preferred not to live,
unless they could live free. Each one of them believed that he was born, not only for his father and
his mother, but for his country also.—And the difference is this.—He who thinks that he is born for
his parents only, waits for his appointed and natural
end: but he who thinks he belongs to his country
also, prefers to die rather than to see her enslaved,
and fears more than death itself, the insults and
dishonor which must be borne when his city is
enthralled.

Were I to assert that it was I who had induced
you to adopt resolves worthy of your ancestors, there
is none who might not justly reprove me. I now
proclaim that these resolves were your own, and that
the same opinions were held by the City before my
time. I only say that some of the credit from each

of these measures should be given to me. But this
fellow, who finds fault with everything, and who is
instigating you to condemn me as the author of all
the City's alarms and calamities, is striving to deprive me, indeed, of this present honor, but is taking
away from you your just eulogy for all time to come.
For if you now convict Ctesiphon by condemning
me as not having pursued the best policy, then will
you appear to have erred, and not to have suffered
what has happened from the injustice of Fortune.
But you have not, you have not erred, Athenians,
in encountering peril for the liberties and safety of
your countrymen. I swear it by the spirits of your
fathers, who went forth to face death at Marathon,
by the men who stood in battle array at Platæa, by
those who fought by sea at Salamis and Artemisium,
by the throng of worthies now reposing in the public
sepulchres,—all gallant men,—all buried by the City
as deserving of the same honor.—Yes, Æschines,
all,—not the victorious and successful only,—all :—
and justly. For all alike did the work of noble
men, and all were subject to the influence of that
fortune which the Divinity assigned to each. And
you, accursed scribe, have been talking of the tro-
phies and battles and great deeds of the olden time,
wishing to rob me of the good opinion and honor of
my countrymen. Which one of those deeds does
this present controversy stand in need of? But, oh
third-rate actor, when the City's leadership of Greece

was in question, in what disposition did it become
me to advise when I arose to speak? Was it to
counsel something unworthy of these our citizens?
—I had been justly put to death had I done so!
—My fellow-citizens, you should in no wise deliberate in the same manner in a private controversy
and upon a public question. In matters of every-
day life you must be governed by the particular facts
and the laws applicable to them; in affairs of State
you must judge in a spirit worthy of your ancestors.
And when you are called to decide public questions,
each one of you, along with his badge and staff of
office, must take up the spirit of the City, if you
deem it your duty to act worthily of your ancestors.

In speaking, however, of the exploits of your forefathers, I have passed over certain decrees and transactions which I now wish to advert to. I therefore
return to the place whence I digressed.

When we reached Thebes we found there Philip's
ambassadors, as well as those of the Thessalians and
the other allies,—our friends dismayed, theirs jubi-
lant. And to prove that I do not say this to aid my
cause, read the letter which our envoys at once sent
home.—This fellow, however, has reached this pitch
of malignity, that whatever succeeds for us, he says,
is the result of fortune, not from me; but if anything
turns out amiss, I and my ill-fortune are the cause.
Thus it seems, I the counsellor and speaker, according to him, have no share in what is counselled or

spoken; while of any disaster to our arms, any defect in generalship, I alone am to be treated as the author. —Where will you find a more brutal or viler calumniator?—But read the letter.

LETTER.*

᾿᾿ When the Assembly met they gave speech first to Philip's ambassadors, on account of their position as allies, and these harangued the people in high praise of Philip, and in abuse of you, rehearsing every hostile act ever done by you against the Thebans. And they summed up by saying that as the Thebans had always experienced kindness from him they should be favorable to Philip,—so, as they had ever been dealt with unjustly by you they should now take satisfaction, as they might prefer,—either by letting loose the allies upon you, or, by invading Attica themselves. And they described, as they thought, the result of their advice, in the number of slaves and cattle and other good things which would be poured into Bœotia; whereas by acting upon our suggestions they would be despoiled in like manner, if the war should take place on Theban soil:—and much more in the same strain.

What we replied to all these things,—to all and each of them,—I would give my life to tell you; but I suppose, as the times have now passed by, you

* No documents are hereafter given, but merely their titles.

would, in the belief that a deluge has swept away
the whole matter, regard what was then said as an
idle tale.   But what we succeeded in obtaining, and
what the Thebans replied to you, now hear.   Take
this letter and read it.

LETTER.

As the result, they sent for and called you to them;
and you departed to their assistance.   To pass over
what occurred in the interim,—they received you so
warmly, that while their own troops were without
the walls, yours were received into the citadel, into
their houses, among their wives and children, and
whatever· they held most precious.   And on that
occasion the Thebans pronounced before the whole
world the highest eulogium upon you, in thus testify-
ing to your courage, your justice, and your temper-
ance.   For in electing to carry on the contest *with*
you, instead of *against* you, they adjudged you to be
both braver and juster in your demands than Philip:
and in acting as they did in regard to what they
and all mankind guard most jealously—their wives
and children—they manifested their confidence in
your virtue.   And in all this, Athenians, they shewed
they judged you rightly.   For after your army entered their city, no one made even an unjust charge
against you, so decorous was your conduct:—and
twice taking part in the first engagements, the one at
the river, and the one during the winter, you shewed

yourselves not only irreproachable, but admirable for
your discipline, your preparation, and your spirit.
Meanwhile praises poured in upon you from others,
and from yourselves processions and sacrifices to the
Gods. And I would here fain ask Æschines whether
whilst this was taking place, and the City was over-
flowing with zeal, and joy, and commendations, he,
too, sacrificed and shared in the general exultation;
or whether he sat still at home grieving and sorrow-
ing and disappointed at the public successes. If he
appeared and took part with the rest, does he not now
act strangely, or rather impiously, if, when he himself at that time called upon the Gods as witnesses to
our success, he would now have you condemn all
this as ill done, after you had invoked the Gods in its
behalf? If he did not then shew himself, is he not
now rightly deserving of many deaths, because while
his fellow-citizens were filled with joy, he was looking with disapproval upon all that was being done?
Read now these decrees.

DECREES.

Whilst we, therefore, were thus joyfully sacrificing,
and the Thebans were convinced they had been saved
by us, it was brought to pass that we, who, through
the machinations of Æschines and his friends, had
seemed to stand in need of assistance, were now
able, by following my advice, to assist others. What
cries Philip uttered, and in what straits he found

himself. in consequence, you shall hear from the letters which he sent into Peloponnesus.. Read them now, that you may see whether my perseverance, and journeys, and efforts, and the numerous decrees which this man has been tearing to pieces, accomplished anything.

Athenians, you have had before my day many distinguished and great orators, the illustrious Callistratus, Aristophon, Kephalus, Thrasybulus, and a thousand others; but none of them gave himself up entirely to the State. He who drew the decree did not go on the embassy, and he who went as ambassador did not write the decree. Each one reserved some indulgence for himself, and in case of reverse some means of recovery. " What, then," shall it be asked, " do you surpass all others in strength and boldness, as if you alone were able to do everything?"—I do not say this:—but I felt the peril which was pressing upon the City to be so great that it seemed to me there was no room to give a thought to individual security, but I must be content to leave nothing undone which ought to be done for the public safety. I was fully persuaded,—perhaps I was wrong,—but I was fully persuaded that no one could write decrees better than I, or do what was to be done, or act as ambassador with more zeal or more uprightness. For these reasons I placed myself in every position. Read now Philip's letters.

15

LETTERS.

, To this condition did my policy reduce Philip,
Æschines; this cry for assistance was he compelled
to utter through my action,—he who before this had
been used to utter threatening speeches against the
City. For this I was justly crowned by my fellow-
citizens, you though present not objecting; and Diondas, who attacked the decree, not obtaining even a
fifth part of the votes. Read me here the decrees
which were absolved by the law, and which this man
did not attack.

DECREES.

· ′ These decrees, Athenians, first written by Aristonicus, recently by Ctesiphon, are in the self-same
words and syllables: and these decrees this Æschines
not only did not attack, but did not even join with
him who did. But if he now assails me fairly, he
might then much more fairly have arraigned Demomeles and Hyperides, who moved the decree.
And why? Because Ctesiphon may well refer to
the decisions of the Courts and to the fact of Æschines not attacking them then although they moved
the very same decrees which Ctesiphon is moving,
and to the laws barring further proceedings in such
cases, and to much more of the like nature.

THEN the question would have been tried upon its
own merits, before any such advantage had been

obtained. THEN, methinks, it could not have been done as he is now doing, raking up from old times and decrees what no one knew of before, nor could have supposed would be referred to to-day for the purpose of slander,—perverting dates, and substituting false motives for the true ones, to give color to what is said. This could not have then been done. For the actual condition of things was then fresh, and you yourselves cognizant of what had taken place; and having, as it were, everything in your hands, those decrees would then have been perfectly understood. But this fellow, avoiding proofs about these matters at the time, comes here at this late day, it seems, thinking you will make this a contest of orators, instead of an inquiry into measures,—a criticism of words, rather than of what was most' profitable to the public.

Then he sophisticates, and says, when you are here as judges you should discard the opinions which you had of us both at home. Just as when you enter upon a reckoning believing there is a surplus, if there is found an exact balance and nothing remains, you acquiesce in the result: so should you now proceed in the same way with the subject in hand. Only look how plainly rotten in its nature is everything which is not fairly done! For, from this sophist's own proposition, you must begin by assuming that I. had been speaking on my country's side, and he on Philip's. He would not try to persuade you to the contrary, unless such was your first impression as to each of us. That he is not acting fairly in asking you to change this opinion I shall shew clearly—not by counters, (that is not the way to deal with public affairs,) but by briefly calling to remembrance each prominent event, and using you who are listening, both as witnesses and reckoners.

My policy, which he condemns, instead of letting the Thebans come swooping down upon your country in concert with Philip, which all expected, fixed them on your side against him;—instead of bringing the war into Attica, kept it seven hundred stadia from your City, on the Theban frontier;—instead of cruisers from Euboea harassing you, Attica was kept free from attack on the sea-side during the whole war;—instead of Philip controlling the Hellespont by taking Byzantium, the Byzantines were on your side against him. Does this seem to be a result like the casting of counters? Is it right, or not, to cancel all these things; or to consider whether they shall not rather be kept in remembrance forever? I do not add, that when Philip became altogether master, it was manifest others had the experience of his harshness; while of his kindness adopted with ulterior views and displayed towards you, you fortunately reaped the fruits. I pass this over altogether.

Moreover, I do not hesitate to say that he who would criticise an orator fairly, and not slander him, does not find fault with such things as this man does, fabricating instances, mimicking my words and personal appearance! Do you not see how very important this is?—The policy of the Greeks is to depend upon whether I made use of this word instead of that, or whether I moved my hand in this direction rather than in that! No! he would have examined the very facts themselves. What resources, what credit had the City when I entered into public life? did I add to them whilst I was in power? and what was the condition of our adversaries? Then, if I had diminished her means the blame would have fallen on me upon his shewing it: if, on the contrary, I had much increased them, he should not have calumniated me. Since you have avoided this course, I shall adopt it. And do you, judges, see that I present my argument fairly.

The resources of the City were confined at that time to some of the islands, and those the weakest; for neither Chios, nor Rhodes, nor Corcyra were with us. The amount of contributions reached but forty-five talents, and even that was anticipated. Of horsemen and foot there were none except the City troops. But the thing most to be dreaded, and which was most favorable to our enemies, was that these men had brought all our neighbors much nearer to a state of hostility than friendliness,—the Megarians, the Thebans, the Eubœans. Such then was our condition, and no one can say it was other-

wise. Look on the other hand at the position of
Philip with whom we were then contending. First
of all, he had the absolute control of his soldiery,
which in war is of the greatest importance. Next,
his troops were always handling their arms;—he
abounded in resources, and his hand was ready to
execute what his head conceived;—he neither proclaimed his views in advance by decrees, nor was he
bound to express them openly, nor was he in dread
of hostile attacks, nor of prosecutions;—in fine, he
was responsible to no one:—he was king, lord,
master. I who was opposed to him, (it is proper
you should consider this too,)—what was I the master
of? Nothing. Even the right to speak I did not
possess exclusively. This right you accorded equally
to those who were in Philip's pay and to me. And
whenever these men prevailed against me, (and
there was much of this as each one found a pretext,)
you went away after really advising in your enemy's
behalf.

Notwithstanding these great disadvantages, I confirmed the Eubœans, the Achæans, the Corinthians,
the Thebans, the Megarians, the Leucadians, and
the Corcyræans, as your allies. They furnished us
fifteen thousand men and two thousand horse over
and above the City's own forces: and I obtained
from them as large a subsidy as I was able. Should
you discuss, Æschines, the fairness of our conditions
with the Thebans, the Byzantines, the Eubœans, and

others, and now find fault with them,—first, you are
ignorant that of the triremes used in the former
naval war by the Greeks,—three hundred in all,—
Athens supplied two hundred. Nor did she think
herself injured by this, or prosecute those who
advised it, or shew displeasure in regard to it,—
(this would have been base,)—but she rather gave
thanks to the Gods that in the common peril of
Greece she was able to furnish twice as many ships
as all the others towards the common safety. Besides, you are bestowing an empty favor upon your
fellow-citizens in slandering me. Why do you now
tell us what should have been done then, when,
although present, you did not state your views, if indeed they were practicable? In the existing juncture
we were obliged to accept not what we desired, but
the best that could then be obtained. There was a
man ready to bid against us, eager to welcome all
who might be driven from us, and prepared to lavish
money to secure his ends.

But if I am now to be blamed for what was actually done, what would you not have heard if, by
reason of my bargaining too closely, the allies had
gone off from us and joined Philip, and he had remained master with Euboea, Thebes, and Byzantium
united to him?

What would not these faithless men have then
done and said? Why, that when the allies wished
to remain with us they had been surrendered and

driven off;—that Philip had got command of the
Hellespont through the Byzantines, and could prevent the transport of food to Greece;—that an op-
pressive border war had been brought directly by
means of the Thebans into Attica;—that the sea
had been closed by the privateers who issued out of
Eubœa.—Would they not have said all this, and
much more of the same kind?

A wicked thing, Athenians, a wicked thing is the
calumniator always, thoroughly censorious and slan-
derous. This fellow, dishonest by nature, is incapable
from the beginning of doing anything straightfor-
ward and liberal: this tragic ape, this rustic Œnomaus, this counterfeit orator! In what has his skill
ever come to his country's aid?—Do you now babble
to us about the past?—Just as if the physician who
had been attending a sick man should give no advice,
nor prescribe anything by which the disease might be
cured, when the patient dies and his funeral is taking
place, should follow him to the tomb, and there cry
out, "If this man had only done thus and so he
would have been alive to-day." Fool! are you now
telling us all this?

You will find, then, that the disasters to the City
which you, wretch that you are, are rejoicing over
instead of lamenting, were in no wise brought about
by me. You should look at it in this light.—Never
up to this time, when I was sent as ambassador by
you, did I return worsted by the ambassadors of

Philip; neither from Thessaly, nor Ambracia, nor ·
from the Illyrians, nor the Thracian kings, nor from
Byzantium, nor from anywhere, nor, last of all, recently from Thebes. But everything in which his
ambassadors were overcome by me in argument,
with arms in his hands he overthrew. Why then
do you demand an account from me of these things,
and why are you not ashamed to sneer at my cowardice, expecting me single-handed to overcome
Philip's power, and this too by words? What else
was I master of? Neither of the spirit of any one,
nor of the fortune of war, nor of the leadership; yet
you demand of me an account of all this,—oblique
and indirect that you are! Of everything which the
statesman should be answerable for, take the fullest
account:—I ask not to be excused. What are these
things?—To watch over the concoction of measures,
to ascertain them even in advance, to proclaim their
scope to the people. All this I did; and everywhere,
the delays, doubts, ignorance, party spirit,—insepa-
rable defects of all our governments,—all these I reduced to a minimum, and even turned to harmony
and union, and to an effort to do what was needed.
Yes, all this I did, and no one ever found anything
in this respect omitted by me.

Should any one ask, by what means then did Philip
obtain his ends; would not all answer, by his army,
by his largesses, by corrupting those in office? I
neither controlled the City's forces, nor the general,

nor am I therefore accountable for anything done in these respects. But in truth I did overmaster Philip when I succumbed not to his offers. For as he who is offering a bribe overcomes the receiver in purchasing him, so the man who does not take the bribe and is not corrupted triumphs over him who attempts to buy him.—In this respect the City never suffered defeat through me.

This is what I furnished to justify the inscription of Ctesiphon's decree concerning me,—this and much more of the same kind. What you yourselves furnished I will now state. Immediately after the battle, the people, knowing and seeing all that I had done, in the midst of their alarm and danger when it would not have been surprising had many of them felt unkindly towards me, took my advice before any other as to the public safety. All that was done in this direction, the ordering of the garrisons, the digging of the trenches, the contribution for the walls, was done under my decrees. Besides, I was elected Commissioner for the supply of food over all competitors.

My enemies immediately, banding together, and plotting my ruin, stirred up against me prosecutions, citations to account, impeachments, and all that sort of thing, not at first through themselves, but principally through others, that they might not be recognized.—For you must surely recollect and know that at that time I was prosecuted almost every day; and

neither the headlong stupidity of Sosicles, the slanders of Philocrates, the madness of Diondas and
Melantus, nor any other expedients were left untried
by them against me. In all these trials I was right-
eously acquitted; first through the favor of the Gods,
next through your sense of justice and that of the
other Athenians. I was declared to have been upright in everything, and this by the verdict of sworn
juries having due regard to their oaths. In the impeachments you not only acquitted me, but you refused the fifth part of your votes to the prosecutors,
so correct did you adjudge my conduct to have been.
In the prosecutions I was shewn both to have counselled and spoken strictly within the law. In the
audits of my accounts you pronounced that my conduct had been in all respects pure and upright. If
all this, then, was so, what title was it becoming or
proper for Ctesiphon to affix to my conduct? Should
it not have been what the people had itself declared?
—what the sworn juries had pronounced?—what
had been adjudged as the truth by every one?

But, says my accuser, what an honorable career
was that of Kephalus,—he never underwent a prosecution at all. And a lucky thing it was for him, by
Jupiter! But is he not as much to be commended
who, though often prosecuted, has never yet been
convicted, and in everything of which he was accused is shewn to have acted uprightly? Nay, more,
Athenians; so far as this Æschines is concerned I

can say what he said of Kephalus; for he himself
never either impeached or prosecuted me. So by .
you yourself I am adjudged to be no whit an inferior
citizen to Kephalus.,

The ill-will and malignity of Æschines we can see
on all sides, but nowhere is it more prominent than
in what he says about fortune. My own opinion is,
that the man who casts up to another his ill-fortune
acts most absurdly. Since when he believes he is
most successful and has his fortune most secure, he
does not know that it will last until evening, how
can he with any propriety plume himself upon it, or
reproach another with his? But since he has spoken
in this way upon many subjects, and is most arrogant
in his contention about this, let us see, Athenians,
whether I shall not express myself with more truth
and humanity about fortune than he has done. I
regard the fortune of the City as good, and I find
that the Dodonean Jupiter has so declared to us; but
the prevailing fortune of every one is at this time
hard and terrible. What Greek, what Barbarian is
not at present suffering most severely? I regard it
especially as part of the City's good fortune that she
chose the nobler part, and so choosing has prospered
more than the very Greeks who thought that in betraying us they would be more successful than we.
To fail sometimes indeed, and not to have everything
succeed as we had expected, is only a part of that
common fatality which the City experienced when it

fell upon us.   My own private fortune or that of any
of us is, in my opinion, to be compared only with the
private fortune of others.   This is my view of the
subject, and is probably also yours; and it seems to
me to be right and proper.   But he who says that
my private fortune should control that of this great
Commonwealth, is comparing a little and insignificant
thing with a great and mighty one.   How can this be ?

If, however, it pleases Æschines to criticise my
fortune, let him look to his own, and if he finds mine
better than his, let him cease carping at it.   Look at
it, then, from the very beginning.   And let no one, in
God's name, think there is anything heartless in my
making this comparison !   I think it most irrational
for any one to insult poverty, or because a man has
been reared in prosperity that he should on that account take honor to himself.   But in consequence of
the vituperations and slanders of this foul-tongued
fellow I am constrained to speak as I am about to
do; I shall endeavor, however, to be as moderate as
I properly can.

I happened, Æschines, when a child to be sent to
proper schools, and to have sufficient means to prevent my resorting to anything base or low.   When
I came to man's estate my conduct was conformable
to my education.   I became choregus, trireme-mas-
ter, and was rated amongst the contributories to the
State's relief.   I shrank from no duty public or
private by which I could be useful either to the City

or my friends. When I afterwards devoted myself
to public affairs, I performed political services for
which I was oftentimes honored with a crown, both
by my own country and the other Greeks : and never
could you my enemies assert that I put my hand to
anything that I should not have properly undertaken.
This is the fortune that has chanced to me; and
although I might say much more about it, I pass it
by, as I wish no one to take offence at my referring
to matters which have been honorable to me.

Let us now consider your fortune, great man that
you are, who have spit upon every one else, and see
what it has been. As a child you were brought up
in penury, attending on the school along with your
father, grinding the ink, sponging the seats, sweep-
ing out the room, and such like menial tasks, not
proper for a free-born youth. When you emerged
from boyhood, you were employed in reading from
the books of your mother the diviner, and the like;
at night, wrapping the initiated in **fawn** skins, pouring water upon them, purifying them, rubbing them
down with clay and bran, raising them after the puri-
fication, and teaching them to chant "*I have avoided
the bad, I have found the good:*" you prided yourself
upon howling as no one else could, and I think myself—don't you, Athenians—that a man who can
harangue so loudly must certainly have been able to
howl sonorously. In the daytime you led strolling
bands along the highways crowned with white poplar

and fennel, pressing the big-jawed serpents, lifting them over your head, bawling out Evoe Saboi, and dancing to the refrain of Hyes Attes, Attes Hyes.

You were also called by the beldames their chorus-leader, rhapsodist, basket-carrier, fan-bearer, and such like names, receiving pay from them in sops, cakes, and rolls. What man would not congratulate himself, truly, upon such a fortune?

You were next enrolled as a citizen,—how I know not, but you were enrolled,—and you immediately chose the noble employment of clerk and servant to some petty official. Removed from this place, in which you did everything you have condemned others for doing,—but not disgracing in it, by Jove, any part of your past life,—you hired yourself to those ranters called actors, Simylus and Socrates. You played third-rate parts with them, picking up the figs and grapes and olives which were thrown at you, and as if you had been a fruit-dealer from the rustic neighborhoods, you made more in this way than from your acting; since you got nothing but knocks from the spectators, from whom you had often to run for your lives. For the war between you and the audience was implacable and relentless. Many hard knocks indeed you carried away with you, and hence you look upon others as cowards who have not had the like experience.

But as it might be urged your poverty was responsible for most of these things, I now turn to the vices of your character itself. You played such a part in public affairs (when you thought of taking to them) that you led the life of a hare, in fear and trembling when your country prospered, and even expecting punishment for the crimes of which you knew yourself guilty:—when adversity overtook us, you strutted forth boldly in the sight of all. The wretch who can take courage from the death of a thousand of his fellow-citizens, what should he not justly suffer at the hands of the survivors? I must omit now much that I had intended to say about him, feeling that I should not mention inconsiderately all that is infamous and disgraceful, but only so much as is not disgraceful for me to speak of.

Let us, however, make a comparison of the circumstances of your life and mine, not rancorously, but with moderation; and then let us ask our fellow-citizens which fortune they would any of them prefer to have.

You taught in schools, I attended them; you assisted at initiations, I was initiated in the highest mysteries; you danced in choruses, I supplied them to the people; you were a petty scribe, I an orator; you acted third-rate parts, I was a spectator; you broke down in them, I hissed; you brought forward measures in favor of our enemies, I for my country: —I omit the rest. To-day I am on trial for a crown, but I am admitted to be guiltless of any crime; while you are shewn to be a libeller and a calumniator, and are even in danger whether you shall continue this trade, or be driven from it by not receiving the fifth part of the votes. A lucky fortune indeed (don't you see) you have enjoyed,—and yet you find fault with mine as bad!

Here now I will read to you the evidence of the services I have rendered to the public, and do you at the same time recite the verses which you once murdered:

"From the drear tombs and darkness' gates I come;"

and

"Ill to proclaim I wish not here to do."

May the Gods bring ill to you, and may your fellow-citizens confound you, wicked citizen and wretched declaimer that you are! Read the evidence.

EVIDENCE.

Such have I been in matters in which the State was concerned. As to my private life, if you do not all know I have ever been kind and liberal, compassionate to the unfortunate, I shall be silent;—I shall neither speak nor offer testimony as to whether I have ransomed citizens from captivity, or supplied marriage portions to their daughters, or the like. This is my view of such things. I am of opinion that while the party obliged should never forget the

16

obligation, he who confers it should dismiss it from his mind, if the one desires to discharge the part of an upright person, and the other of a man of honor. To bring to remembrance and to proclaim one's acts of beneficence differs little from reproaching the recipient. I shall not do this, nor can I be forced to it. However I may be thought of in this respect, I am well content.

Having now passed altogether from private matters, I wish to say a few words more about public.

If you can now shew, Æschines, that a human· being under the sun, Greek or Barbarian, has not suffered wrong, first from the rule of Philip, afterwards from that of Alexander, I will give up to you my fortune—or my ill-fortune, if you choose to call it so—as the cause of all. If, on the other hand, people who have never looked upon me or heard me speak have been all grievously injured,—not merely individuals, but whole communities and nations,— how much more fair and true does it seem, that to the common lot of humanity—some cruel course of events like nothing ever seen—should be attributed the happening of these disasters! Disregarding this, however, you condemn me and my policy, when it is apparent that the whole blame, or at least a heavy part of it, should fall upon all, and upon you in par- ticular. Let it be granted that I obtained the sole control of affairs, was it not open to all of you to attack me? And if you were always present in our assemblies, and the City looked to the public discussion of what was best for her interests, and then my counsels appeared best to all, and to none more than you, (for from no kindness to me did you surrender your hopes, the public esteem, and your honors to my propositions—thus shewing you were vanquished by the truth, and had nothing better to offer,) what a monstrous wrong and injustice are you not now committing in condemning measures than which you could then propose nothing more useful!

See how this question is settled by the opinion of the whole world. Does a man purposely do wrong, he is the object of anger and punishment. Does he simply err unwittingly, pardon and not punishment is extended to him. Has a man undertaken to devote himself to what seemed to be the public good, and, without dishonesty or fault, failed in common with every one else; it is unjust either to punish or blame him,—he is the object of sympathy. This is clear not only from the written law, but from the unwritten law of nature and man's moral constitution. But Æschines so far exceeds every one in cruelty and malignity that the very things which he once looked upon as misfortunes to me he now imputes as crimes.

Then with a seeming air of candor and kindness he has asked you to watch and keep your eyes upon me, lest I might deceive and beguile you; calling me a wonderful speaker, a trickster, a sophist, and the like; and in this way by first attributing to another his own bad qualities, he prevents his hearers from inquiring into the character of him who brings the charge. But I am sure you all see through this fellow, and are convinced that these vices are a part of his own nature and not of mine. For I know full well that my skill in oratory,—(I suppose I have some skill in speaking, although I am convinced it is the hearers who are usually the masters of the speaker's power, for according as you regard and shew kindness to him, do his talents seem to display themselves,—) if then I possess this faculty, you have always found it exerted for your advantage in public affairs, never against you, or for my private ends. Æschines, on the other hand, has either been always speaking in behalf of your enemies, or against those he thought had injured or offended him. Never has he employed his talents in the cause of justice, or for the State's advantage. An upright citizen should never ask the judges assembled in the public interest to consider and pass upon his private griefs and animosities; nor should he even approach them on such subjects: least of all should he have such feelings in his heart,—or if he cannot help this, they should be held in moderation, and under control.

On what occasions then should the statesman and the orator be vehement?—When some vital interest of his country is in danger, or in matters urged against the public enemy.—In such cases, properly:—for they much concern the zealous and the honest citizen. But when of no *public* wrong, and I aver of no *private* one, he ever justly accused me,—neither against the City nor himself,—to be getting up an accusation as to whether I should be crowned and honored, and to be expending this flood of words,—*this* is indeed an exhibition of private hatred and malice, the mark of a mean spirit, not of an honorable man.—And if he declines a direct encounter with me, attacking in form another, this is the very depth of baseness.

You seem to me thus, Æschines, from your conduct, to have undertaken this accusation to make a display of your rhetoric and your fine voice, not for the punishment of any crime. But it is not the language of the orator or the tone of his voice which are held in value, but the choice of what is acceptable to one's fellow-citizens, the hating and loving as our country does. The orator with such feelings will say everything with honest warmth. He who cherishes those from whom the City apprehends danger, does not ride upon the same anchor with his fellow-citizens, for he can never have the same expectation of safety with them. But—do you see?—I have; for I have always adopted a course conformable with my country's interest, nor had I ever anything separate and apart from her. Is that so with you? How can it be? Immediately after the battle, you went as ambassador to Philip the cause of all our City's woes, and yet, as all men know, you had formerly refused this office. Who then has deceived the City? Is it not he who does not say what he thinks? Whom does the herald justly denounce at the opening of our Assemblies? Is it not such a man as this? What heavier accusation can be brought against a public man than that his tongue does not utter the thoughts which are in his heart? You have been proved to be such a man.

And yet you lift up your voice loudly here, and dare to look upon the faces of your fellow-citizens! As if they do not know who you are! As if they are all in such a state of stupor and oblivion as not to remember the words which you publicly pronounced when you asserted and asseverated there was no connection between you and Philip, and that I had, contrary to the truth, so charged against you on account of private enmity! Scarcely had the news of the battle been proclaimed, when, forgetting all this, you instantly confessed and laid claim to a friendship and intimacy with Philip, by those names covering up the hire and salary you had taken from him. With what propriety, Æschines, can you assert that Philip was ever host, friend, or intimate of the son of Glaucothea the timbrel-player! I shall never believe it. You were bribed to bring to nought everything which might have availed your country, and yet, standing confest a traitor, and a self-convicted libeller, you attack and charge me forsooth for things of which you well know any one is rather the cause than I.

Many and great things, Æschines, has the City undertaken and succeeded in through me, and of this she has never been unmindful. Here is a proof. When the citizens, immediately after the fatal event, were about to choose an orator to pronounce the oration over those who had fallen, they neither selected you although put forward on account of your fine voice, nor Demades although he had just negotiated the peace, nor Hegemon, nor any of you, but ME. And notwithstanding you and Pythocles came forward, and, oh Jupiter and all the Gods, savagely and ruthlessly attacked me, accusing me of the same things you have urged against me to-day, they all the more selected me! You are not ignorant of the reason, but I will tell you all the same. The people had witnessed the devotion and good-will with which I administered their affairs, and at the same time your misconduct and dishonesty. What you had openly disavowed with protestations when our affairs were prosperous, in the City's adversity you openly professed. Those, therefore, who found safety for their opinions in the public distress, the people looked upon as their enemies from the first, as they had now shewn themselves so when occasion offered. Moreover, they thought it more becoming that he who was to pronounce the funeral oration, and was to celebrate the valor of the men who had fallen, should not have lived under the same roof and drunk of the same cup with those who had been arrayed against them;—that those who had rejoiced and sung pæans over yonder upon the misfortunes of Greece with the authors of her ruin, should not come forward here to be honored;—that the orator should not feign to weep over their fate with his voice only, but should grieve from his heart. This they felt was the case with *themselves*, with *me*, but not with *you*. Such were the reasons why I was chosen, and not you. And not only did the people thus act, but the fathers and brothers of the slain selected by the people to discharge the funeral rites, did the same thing. For when it became necessary that the funeral banquet should be provided, it was given not at the house of any kinsman of the deceased, as is usually done, but at mine. And properly. For while each of them was nearer to each of his fallen kinsmen than I, none was nearer to them all than I, in the common grief. He who had the greatest interest in their success and preservation, he indeed had the greatest share of grief in what all felt for their undeserved fate.

Read him the epitaph which the City ordered to be inscribed at the public expense, that you may see in it, Æschines, what a malevolent foul-mouthed rogue you are. Read it, I say.

EPITAPH.

" Here lie who fought their country's rights t' uphold,
And strove to quell the foe's proud insolence.

> Valor and spirit nought availed, they fell,
> And to the common Judge, grim Pluto, passed.
> From slavery's hated yoke the Grecian neck
> To guard, they gave their lives. Their mother Earth
> Her children's precious bodies loving holds ;
> Since the decree from Jove is sent, to whom
> Alone belongs in all things to succeed,
> Never to fail. Man cannot fly from Fate."

Do you hear, Æschines ?—in this very epitaph it is said, to the Gods alone belong success, and not to fail. Not to the counsellor is it given to cause the combatants to succeed, but to the Gods alone. Why, then, wicked wretch, do you blame me for this ill-success, and charge me with disasters which may the Gods let fall upon the heads of you and yours !

Whilst this man was falsely charging me with many crimes, Athenians, I was particularly struck with this ;—that while he was passing in review the calamities with which the City had from time to time been afflicted, he never shewed the disposition of a loyal or friendly citizen,—he neither shed tears nor in any way expressed sympathy with his country's distresses. But when he raised his voice, and loudly harangued with an air of satisfaction, and thought to condemn me altogether, he bore testimony against himself, inasmuch as he did not exhibit in our misfortunes the same feelings as the rest of us. It seems to me that when a man is pretending to take an interest in our laws and frame of government, as he has been doing, he should at least be able, if nothing else, to grieve and rejoice over the same things with his fellow-citizens, and not to range himself by his public conduct in the class, of their opponents as he has been doing. Æschines has just declared that I was the cause of everything, and that through me all the State's recent disasters were brought about; but it was never through my advice, or by my prompting, that you, my fellow-citizens, first began to assist the other Greeks. If, indeed, you should give me the credit that it was through me you had been first brought to oppose the power arrayed against the Greeks, it would truly be a greater honor than you have ever yet conferred upon any one. But I do not say this, (I should be unjust to you if I did,) and I well know you would never make such a concession; and my antagonist, had he acted honestly, would never from hostility to me have thus tarnished and defaced one of your most glorious achievements.

But why do I call him to account for this, when he has wickedly charged me with a much more infamous crime? He has charged me,—heavens and earth, what will he not say next,—with Philippizing! By Hercules and all the Gods, if we consider this matter accurately, inquiring fairly and without hatred who the persons are who in very truth may be described as the cause of these disasters, it will be found they are persons in each Grecian State, like Æschines, and not any who thought as I did;—persons who, when Philip's power was feeble and at a low ebb, and whilst we were counselling and advising, and preparing the best measures, abandoned from a sordid greed for money what was best for the public good, and deceived and corrupted their respective countrymen until they had enslaved them.— Such men were Daochus, Kineas, Thrasylaus, with the Thessalians; Kercidas, Hieronymus, Eucampidas, with the Arcadians; Myrtis, Teledamus, Mnaseas, with the Argives; Euxitheus, Cleotimus, Aristæchmus, with the Eleans; Neon and Thrasylochus, sons of the accursed Philiades, with the Messenians; Aristratus, Epichares, with the Sykionians; Dinarchus, Demaratus, with the Corinthians; Ptœodorus, Helixus, Perilaus, with the Megarians; Timolaus, Theogiton, Anemœtas, with the Thebans; Hipparchus, Clitarchus, Sosistratus, with the Eubœans :— the day would fail me to enumerate even the names of these traitors. Those, Athenians, those were men, all like-minded in their own country with these wretches in ours, vile flatterers, accursed parasites who have maimed and mutilated their respective States, pledging away their liberties first to Philip, afterwards to Alexander; who place their happiness in their bellies, and the gratification of the lowest sensuality, and who have brought to ruin that freedom and that spirit which refused to own a master, and which to the Greeks of old were the boundaries and canons of everything that was good.

Of this base and infamous arrangement, or to speak in earnest, Athenians, of this betrayal of the liberties of Greece, Athens through my counsels is guiltless in the eyes of men; and I in yours. If you ask then again, Æschines, for what services I deem myself worthy of honor from my country, I answer that when all the public men of Greece were being corrupted, beginning with yourself, first by Philip, afterwards by Alexander, neither opportunity, nor fair words, nor mighty promises, nor hopes, nor fears, nor anything, inclined or moved me to yield a jot of what I thought just and useful to my country. What I advised the State to do, I did not, like you and your fellows, advise, throwing self-interest, as in a balance, into the scales to depress them; but I did everything fairly, honestly, and with a heart that was incorruptible. And controlling larger affairs than any man of my time, I managed all with purity, uprightness, and discretion.—Therefore do I claim to be honored.

As to the walls which you sneer at, and the intrenchments, I consider them also deserving of praise and gratitude;—why are they not?—I place them, however, nowhere near my acts of administration. I did not merely surround the City with walls of stone and bricks,—I do not take credit to myself chiefly on this account. If you will look fairly at the fortifications which I erected, you will find them in the arms, and cities, and strong places, and harbors, and ships,

and horses, and men, which I secured to Athens.
These were the bulwarks with which I protected
Attica, doing everything which human counsel could
perform: in this way I walled the whole country
round about, not merely the circuit of the Piræus, or
of the citadel.   By Philip's calculations and preparations never was I defeated,—far from it;—the generals and forces of the allies were vanquished by
Fate.   Do you ask for the proofs?   They are plain
and clear as the day.—Look at them.

PROOFS.

What should the well-affected statesman have done
who was providing with the utmost care and zeal and
solicitude for the interests of Athens?   Should it not
have been to defend Attica on the sea-side by Eubœa,
in the middle by Bœotia, and on the side of Peloponnesus by the contiguous States?—To provide for the
transport of corn until passing along a friendly coast
it should reach Piræus itself?—To preserve the places
which belonged to us by sending advice and assistance
for their succor,—Proconnesus, Chersonnesus, and
Tenedos;—and draw into friendship and alliance
Byzantium, Abydos, and Eubœa?—To weaken and
cut off the supplies of the enemy, and to procure
what the City most stood in need of?—All these
things were done by my measures and through my
decrees; and all, Athenians, if not looked at in an
envious spirit, will be found to have been well done,

—with the utmost rectitude,—the favorable opportunity never lost, nor omitted, nor cast away; and so far as lay within the power and faculties of a single man, nothing left undone. But if either the enmity of some deity, or the power of fortune, or the want of skill in our generals, or the treachery of those who betrayed your cities, or all these things together, made havoc with your affairs until they were entirely ruined, why is Demosthenes in fault?

Had there been in each Grecian city a man such as I was towards you; or had there been even but a single man in Thessaly and another in Arcadia like-minded as myself, no one either outside the Gates of Greece, or within them, would have suffered the present distresses; but all the Greeks would have been independent ànd self-governing, and dwelt in their respective countries in happiness, security, and freedom from alarm, thanking you and the other Athenians, through me, for these benefits. And that you may see how much these advantages outweigh my words, in a desire to avoid envy I ask you to read this list of aids to our country which were obtained by my decrees.

ENUMERATION OF AIDS.

Such things, Æschines, it becomes the patriotic and good citizen to do, and by succeeding in them, heavens and earth, we should have been undoubtedly the greatest of people, and deservedly;—even in failure our conduct has been glorious, none can blame the City, or its policy, but Fortune alone which had so ordered;—but never will he abstain from assisting his country, nor sell himself to her enemies, nor serve their interests against her. Nor upon him who is urging and preparing measures in favor of his country and striving to stand fast by them will he look with hatred; nor if any one has privately offended him, will he treasure it up and nurse it. Nor will he maintain an unjust and treacherous retirement, as you have often done:—for there is a proper retirement, profitable to the City, which many of you have fairly maintained. But such has not been Æschines's withdrawal from public life—far from it; retiring whenever he pleased,—and that was often enough,—he watched the opportunity when you were wearied with listening to the same adviser, or when some stroke of ill-fortune had befallen you, or something adverse had occurred,—so often the case in human affairs,—then seizing the occasion he started up from his seclusion, and shewed himself like a tempest. And with cadenced tones he rolled out words and sentences, stringing them together without stopping for breath, although they brought with them no advantage or offer of relief to the State,—but only ruin to some of our citizens, and disgrace to all. Yet of such care and attention, Æschines, if inspired by an honest heart and a desire to serve the State, the fruits should be valuable, and serviceable, and honorable, such as alliances with other cities, the supply of means, the opening of commercial markets, the enactment of useful laws, the hindrance of our known enemies. Such in past times was what was expected, and the past gave many opportunities of proving this to the honorable and upright man. On those occasions you were neither first, nor second, nor third, nor fourth, nor fifth, nor sixth, nor in any place at all; never, certainly on any occasion by which your country was benefited.

What alliances did the City ever procure through you? What aid, what increase of glory or esteem? What embassy, what service by which the City was placed in a better position? What matter which you controlled, either at home or with the other Greeks, or with foreigners, was ever brought to a successful conclusion by your agency? What ships, what military engines, what docks, what construction of walls, what horsemen, in what of any of these things have you ever been serviceable? What assistance, from public spirit or liberality, was ever rendered by you to rich or poor? None. If nothing of this kind, when did you ever shew kindness or affection? Where, when? Most heartless of men, while every one who has ever spoken from this place has contributed to the relief of his fellow-citizens,— Aristonicus giving away recently the very money which had been set apart to restore him to his civic privileges,—you have never given or contributed aught. You were not without means, how could you be? You inherited from Philo, your father-in-law, more than five talents, not to speak of the two talents you got from the heads of the symmories for mutilating to their relief the law concerning the trierarchs. But that I may not, passing from one thing to another, elude the present question, I leave these matters. It is clear you were not prevented from giving by want of means; but because you took good care never to act in any way against those friends of yours to whom you were subservient in everything. In what, then, are you bold and zealous, and when are you conspicuous? When it is necessary to speak against your fellow-citizens:—then your voice is loud and clear, and your memory perfect, oh, best of actors, tragic Theocrines!

You have reminded us, Æschines, of the mighty men of old, and it is well:—but it is not just, Athenians, that my opponent should take the gratitude you now feel towards those patriots, and use it against me by a contrast of the living with the dead. For who does not know that an overmastering and belittling envy is always at work against the living, while the dead cease to be hated even by their enemies? If such be human nature, shall I be judged and compared with those who have gone before me? By no means; this is neither fair nor just. Com-

17

pare me with yourself, Æschines, or with whom you please of those who think as you do who are now living.

Moreover, consider this. Is it better and more profitable to the State, on account of the enormous and immeasurably great services of our ancestors, to treat the well-meant efforts of contemporary actors with thanklessness and derision, or to award the meed of praise to all who strive to do well in its behalf? But can I not say that my advice and my policy when rightly looked at is of like character and essentially the same as that of those illustrious men; and that yours is of a piece with that of their calumniators? It is clear that in their time too there were those who maligned the living, and who besmeared the men of the past with praise,—a base act, and what you are now doing.

You assert then that I am totally unlike those men. But are you like them, Æschines, or your brother? Or any of your orators? I say not one.

Compare me, honest declaimer, (for I shall call you nothing else,) with the living, compare the living with his competitors as in other cases,—as with poets, with musicians, with wrestlers. Philammon, although he was not so strong as Glaucus the Caristian and other athletes who had gone before him, never returned uncrowned from the Olympian Games; for since he excelled all with whom he contended, he went forth crowned and triumphant. Match me then with the

Statesmen of to-day, with yourself, with any one you please.—I except none.

When the Commonwealth was able to choose the best course, and when to strive for its advantage in public affairs was a matter of emulation with all, I counselled most wisely, and by my decrees and my laws and my embassies everything was directed; and you, none of you, were to be found anywhere, unless it was necessary to do the State a mischief. When adversity came, and there was no longer a searching out for counsellors, but for men who were working for those behind them, who were ready to prostitute themselves for pay against their country, and to flatter the stranger, then you, and your fellows came forth radiant, and great, and splendid,—and I, I admit it, was very low, but still your friend,—while these men were not.

Two qualities, Athenians, an upright statesman should possess,—and I thus speak as I am speaking of myself to avoid being invidious,—when in power, he should advocate a policy both honorable and lofty; and at all times, and in all contingencies, he should be loyal to his country. This last quality is native to the heart,—power and strength depend upon other things,—and this last you have always found abiding in me. Although my person was demanded by the stranger, although cited before the Amphictyonic Council, although harassed by many prosecutions, although hounded by these miscreants who pursued

Lightning Source UK Ltd.
Milton Keynes UK
UKHW021235301118
333254UK00009B/483/P

9 781332 037322